GEORG SIMMEL

Conflict

AND

The Web of Group-Affiliations

GEORG SIMMEL

Conflict

TRANSLATED BY KURT H. WOLFF

The Web of Group-Affiliations

TRANSLATED BY REINHARD BENDIX

WITH A FOREWORD BY EVERETT C. HUGHES

THE FREE PRESS

GLENCOE, ILLINOIS

Contents

881274

Foreword

KURT H. WOLFF AND THE FREE PRESS did American scholars a distinct service by translating and publishing important parts of the sociological work of Georg Simmel in a volume entitled *The Sociology of Georg Simmel* (1950). Reinhard Bendix has joined them in a further service by making an additional chapter of Simmel's *Soziologie* available. Their contribution is made the greater by the fact that those Americans whose mother-tongue is English (including those among them whose mother's tongue was not English) are extremely loath to learn other languages. Translations from other languages are also relatively few and are slow in appearing. If we should now stop the stream of immigrants of some measure of higher learning acquired in other languages, our linguistic isolation may become even more embarrassing than it is now. We are already peculiarly dependent upon translations.

The major intellectual danger of this dependence is that we Americans will often simply not know of work written in other languages. A minor danger is that we may take the translated part for the whole of a man's work. This second risk is much reduced, for Simmel's work, by the appearance of the crucial chapters which make up this volume. As a matter of fact, Simmel's work is less subject to this danger than is that of many scolars. For his style of thought shines clearly through in nearly every piece of his writing, even in many of the smaller essays which he wrote for magazines and for the feature sections of newspapers. But if less is lost by reading only a small part of his work, it does not follow that there is less gain in reading more. Quite the contrary, for his pages are so full of brilliant insights, and of applications of his style of analysis to concrete cases, that the reward for reading on and on is especially great.

One might apply to Simmel's work his own dialectic of form and content. The basic form of his thought is recognizable in almost any small part of his work, but it is elaborated in being applied to each new content. And since, as he says, content and form are relative terms, every new content enables him to raise the level of abstraction with which he conceives social forms; but the higher the level of abstraction, the richer the variety of contents suggested by the form and the greater the number of facets of social reality perceived through it. Simmel's thought nearly completes its circle again and again; but just as the circle is about to be closed, his thought takes wing in some new arc that almost becomes another circle. This gives his work a tentative, never quite complete, which some mistake for an unsystematic, quality.

Critics of Simmel say that he never proves anything by empirical test. That is true. As his thought develops, he flashes an illustration before us; say, the Catholic clergy. The clergy gives him a model (ideal-type or pure case) of a social group which, although it draws its postulants from all classes and nations, is free of all complicating overlapping memberships. Celibacy frees the postulants from their past and keeps their present uncomplicated. The case is an example, and a stimulus to thought, not a demonstration. It may not even be a true example of the form he describes. But his case will suggest others which approximate the form in question; and approximations can be tested as absolutes never can be.

In Simmel, movement from pure model (form) to particular case (content) and back again is incomparably more rapid than in any other of the classic sociologists. The variety of both forms and contents presented for analysis and illustrations is correspondingly greater. If he is wrong in fact more often than others (I do not say that he is), it is because he alludes to a greater variety of fact, of times, places and circumstances. Until we can do much better than we now do at fitting data to the needs of insights and ideas (much of our present empirical ingenuity is exerted in exactly the opposite direction) we will do well to temper our criticism of Simmel's fashion of illustrating his ideas by examples drawn from wide historical knowledge and great social sophistication rather than testing them by experiment or controlled observation.

The title of this volume is *Conflct* and *The Web of Group-Affiliations*. It might well have borne also the sub-title: *Essays on Social Organization*. For Simmel sees conflict as part of the dynamic by which some men are drawn together (and others, by the same token, driven away from each other) into those uneasy combinations which we call groups. The inter-weaving or, better, the entangling of social circles (group formation and group affiliations in Bendix' translation) is viewed, in the same way, as part of the dynamic both of groups and of the individual personalities who compose them. Simmel is thus the Freud of the study of society. Instead of seeing change as disturbance of a naturally stable thing called society, he sees stability itself as some temporary (although it may long endure) balance among forces in interaction; and forces are by definition capable of being described only in terms of change. This is strikingly similar to what Freud did for the study of human personality. Like Freud, he has many intellectual children. Not all of them have that wisdom which makes them know their own father.

EVERETT CHERRINGTON HUGHES

Conflict[1]

TRANSLATED BY KURT H. WOLFF

1. The title of this essay is *Der Streit*. "*Streit*" is usually translated as "quarrel," but has a broader meaning for Simmel; hence "conflict" seems better. The essay is Chapter 4 of Soziologie (1908); it is translated from the third edition of this work (1923; pp. 186-255). All sub-headings are supplied, as are passages in brackets. An earlier translation of a considerably different original by Albion W. Small ("The Sociology of Conflict," *The American Journal of Sociology*, Vol. IX, 1904), has been examined, but is not the basis of the present rendition. For a fuller bibliographical reference to Small's translation, see *The Sociology of Georg Simmel*, transl., ed., and with an introd. by Kurt H. Wolff (Glencoe, Illinois: The Free Press, 1950), p. lviii.–Tr.

Chapter One

The Sociological Nature
of Conflict

CONFLICT AS SOCIATION

THE SOCIOLOGICAL SIGNIFICANCE of conflict (*Kampf*) has in principle never been disputed. Conflict is admitted to cause or modify interest groups, unifications, organizations. On the other hand, it may sound paradoxical in the common view if one asks whether irrespective of any phenomena that result from conflict or that accompany it, it itself is a form of sociation.[2] At first glance, this sounds like a rhetorical question. If every interaction among men is a sociation, conflict—after all one of the most vivid interactions, which, furthermore, cannot possibly be carried on by one individual alone—must certainly be considered as sociation. And in fact, *dis*sociating factors—hate, envy, need, desire—are the *causes* of conflict; it breaks out because of them. Conflict is thus designed to resolve divergent dualisms; it is a way of achieving some kind of unity, even if it be through the annihilation of one of the conflicting parties. This is roughly parallel to the fact that it is the most violent symptom of a disease which represent the effort of the organism to free itself of disturbances and damages caused by them.

But this phenomenon means much more than the trivial "*si vis pacem para bellum*" [if you want peace, prepare for

---

2. "*Vergesellschaftungsform.*" "*Vergesellschaftung*" will be rendered as "sociation." On the term and its various translations, see *The Sociology of Georg Simmel, loc. cit.*, pp. lxiii-lxiv.—Tr.

war]; it is something quite general, of which this maxim only describes a special case. Conflict itself resolves the tension between contrasts. The fact that it aims at peace is only one, an especially obvious, expression of its nature: the synthesis of elements that work both against and for one another. This nature appears more clearly when it is realized that both forms of relation—the antithetical and the convergent—are fundamentally distinguished from the mere indifference of two or more individuals or groups. Whether it implies the rejection or the termination of sociation, indifference is purely negative. In contrast to such pure negativity, conflict contains something positive. Its positive and negative aspects, however, are integrated; they can be separated conceptually, but not empirically.

THE SOCIOLOGICAL RELEVANCE
OF CONFLICT

SOCIAL PHENOMENA appear in a new light when seen from the angle of this sociologically positive character of conflict. It is at once evident then that if the relations among men (rather than what the individual is to himself and in his relations to objects) constitute the subject matter of a special science, sociology, then the traditional topics of that science cover only a subdivision of it: it is more comprehensive and is truly defined by a principle. At one time it appeared as if there were only two consistent subject matters of the science of man: the individual unit and the unit of individuals (society); any third seemed logically excluded. In this conception, conflict itself—irrespective of its contributions to these immediate social units—found no place for study. It was a phenomenon of its own, and its subsumption under the concept of unity would have been arbitrary as well as useless, since conflict meant the negation of unity.

A more comprehensive classification of the science of the

relations of men should distinguish, it would appear, those relations which constitute a unit, that is, social relations in the strict sense, from those which counteract unity.[3] It must be realized, however, that both relations can usually be found in every historically real situation. The individual does not attain the unity of his personality exclusively by an exhaustive harmonization, according to logical, objective, religious, or ethical norms, of the contents of his personality. On the contrary, contradiction and conflict not only precede this unity but are operative in it at every moment of its existence. Just so, there probably exists no social unit in which convergent and divergent currents among its members are not inseparably interwoven. An absolutely centripetal and harmonious group, a pure "unification" ("*Vereinigung*"), not only is empirically unreal, it could show no real life process. The society of saints which Dante sees in the Rose of Paradise may be like such a group, but it is without any change and development; whereas the holy assembly of Church Fathers in Raphael's *Disputa* shows if not actual conflict, at least a considerable differentiation of moods and directions of thought, whence flow all the vitality and the really organic structure of that group. Just as the universe needs "love and hate," that is, attractive and repulsive forces, in order to have any form at all, so society, too, in order to attain a determinate shape, needs some quantitative ratio of harmony and disharmony, of association and competition, of favorable and unfavorable tendencies. But these discords are by no means mere sociological liabilities or negative instances. Definite, actual society does not result only from other social forces which are positive, and only to the extent that the negative factors do not hinder them. This common conception is quite superficial: society, as we know it, is the result of both cate-

---

3. "*Einheit*" is both "unit" and "unity," and Simmel uses the term promiscuously in both senses.—Tr.

gories of interaction, which thus both manifest themselves as wolly positive.[4]

UNITY AND DISCORD

THERE IS a misunderstanding according to which one of these two kinds of interaction tears down what the other builds up, and what is eventually left standing is the result of the subtraction of the two (while in reality it must rather be

---

4. This is the sociological instance of a contrast between two much more general conceptions of life. According to the common view, life always shows two parties in opposition. One of them represents the positive aspect of life, its content proper, if not its substance, while the very meaning of the other is non-being, which must be subtracted from the positive elements before they can constitute life. This is the common view of the relation between happiness and suffering, virtue and vice, strength and inadequacy, success and failure—between all possible contents and interruptions of the course of life. The highest conception indicated in respect to these contrasting pairs appears to me different: we must conceive of all these polar differentiations as of *one* life; we must sense the pulse of a central vitality even in that which, if seen from the standpoint of a particular ideal, ought not to be at all and is merely something negative; we must allow the total meaning of our existence to grow out of *both* parties. In the most comprehensive context of life, even that which as a single element is disturbing and destructive, is wholly positive; it is not a gap but the fulfillment of a role reserved for it alone. Perhaps it is not given to us to attain, much less always to maintain, the height from which all phenomena can be felt as making up the unity of life, even though from an objective or value standpoint, they appear to oppose one another as pluses and minuses, contradictions, and mutual eliminations. We are too inclined to think and feel that our essential being, our true, ultimate significance, is identical with one of these factions. According to our optimistic or pessimistic feeling of life, one of them appears to us as surface or accident, as something to be eliminated or subtracted, in order for the true and intrinsically consistent life to emerge. We are everywhere enmeshed in this dualism (which will presently be discussed in more detail in the text above)—in the most intimate as in the most comprehensive provinces of life, personal, objective, and social. We think we have, or are, a whole or unit which is composed of two logically and objectively opposed parties, and we identify this totality of ours with one of them, while we feel the other to be something alien which does not properly belong and which denies our central and comprehensive being. Life constantly moves between these two tendencies. The one has just been described. The other lets the whole really *be* the whole. It makes the unity, which after all comprises both contrasts, alive in each of these contrasts and in their juncture. It is all the more necessary to assert the right of this second tendency in respect to the sociological phenomenon of conflict, because conflict impresses us with its socially destructive force as with an apparently indisputable fact.

designated as the result of their addition). This misunderstanding probably derives from the twofold meaning of the concept of unity. We designate as "unity" the consensus and concord of interacting individuals, as against their discords, separations, and disharmonies. But we also call "unity" the total group-synthesis of persons, energies, and forms, that is, the ultimate wholeness of that group, a wholeness which covers both strictly-speaking unitary relations and dualistic relations. We thus account for the group phenomenon which we feel to be "unitary" in terms of functional components considered *specifically* unitary; and in so doing, we disregard the other, larger meaning of the term.

This imprecision is increased by the corresponding twofold meaning of "discord" or "opposition." Since discord unfolds its negative, destructive character between particular individuals, we naïvely conclude that it must have the same effect on the total group. In reality, however, something which is negative and damaging between individuals if it is considered in isolation and as aiming in a particular direction, does not necessarily have the same effect within the total relationship of these individuals. For, a very different picture emerges when we view the conflict in conjunction with other interactions not affected by it. The negative and dualistic elements play an entirely positive role in this more comprehensive picture, despite the destruction they may work on particular relations. All this is very obvious in the competition of individuals within an economic unit.

CONFLICT AS AN INTEGRATIVE FORCE IN THE GROUP

HERE, among the more complex cases, there are two opposite types. First, we have small groups, such as the marital couple, which nevertheless involve an unlimited number of vital relations among their members. A certain amount of discord, inner divergence and outer controversy, is organically tied up with the very elements that ultimately hold the group together; it cannot be separated from the unity of the sociological structure. This is true not only in cases of evident marital failure but also in marriages characterized by a *modus vivendi* which is bearable or at least borne. Such marriages are not "less" marriages by the amount of conflict they contain; rather, out of so many elements, among which there is that inseparable quantity of conflict, they have developed into the definite and characteristic units which they are. Secondly, the positive and integrating role of antagonism is shown in structures which stand out by the sharpness and carefully preserved purity of their social divisions and gradations. Thus, the Hindu social system rests not only on the hierarchy, but also directly on the mutual repulsion, of the castes. Hostilities not only prevent boundaries within the group from gradually disappearing, so that these hostilities are often consciously cultivated to guarantee existing conditions. Beyond this, they also are of direct sociological fertility: often they provide classes and individuals with reciprocal positions which they would not find, or not find in the same way, if the causes of hostility were not accompanied by the *feeling* and the expression of hostility—even if the same objective causes of hostility were in operation.

The disappearance of repulsive (and, considered in isolation, destructive) energies does by no means always result in a richer and fuller social life (as the disappearance of liabilities results in larger property) but in as different and unrealizable a phenomenon as if the group were deprived of the forces of cooperation, affection, mutual aid, and harmony of interest. This is not only true for competition generally, which determines the form of the group, the reciprocal positions of its participants, and the distances between them, and which does so purely as a formal matrix of tensions, quite irrespective of its objective *results*. It is true also where the group is based on the attitudes of its members. For instance, the opposition of a member to an associate is no purely negative social factor, if only because such opposition is often the only means for making life with actually unbearable people at least possible. If we did not even have the power and the right to rebel against tyranny, arbitrariness, moodiness, tactlessness, we could not bear to have any relation to people from whose characters we thus suffer. We would feel pushed to take desperate steps—and these, indeed, would end the relation but do *not*, perhaps, constitute "conflict." Not only because of the fact (though it is not essential here) that oppression usually increases if it is suffered calmly and without protest, but also because opposition gives us inner satisfaction, distraction, relief, just as do humility and patience under different psychological conditions. Our opposition makes us feel that we are not completely victims of the circumstances. It allows us to prove our strength consciously and only thus gives vitality and reciprocity to conditions from which, without such corrective, we would withdraw at any cost.

Opposition achieves this aim even where it has no noticeable success, where it does not become manifest but remains purely covert. Yet while it has hardly any practical effect, it may yet achieve an inner balance (sometimes even on the part of *both* partners to the relation), may exert a quieting influence, produce a feeling of virtual power, and thus save relationships whose continuation often puzzles the observer. In such cases, opposition is an element in the relation itself; it is intrinsically interwoven with the other reasons for the relation's existence. It is not only a *means* for preserving the relation but one of the concrete functions which actually constitute it. Where relations are purely external and at the same time of little practical significance, this function can be satisfied by conflict in its *latent* form, that is, by aversion and feelings of mutual alienness and repulsion which upon more intimate contact, no matter how occasioned, immediately change into positive hatred and fight.

Without such aversion, we could not imagine what form modern urban life, which every day brings everybody in contact with innumerable others, might possibly take. The whole inner organization of urban interaction is based on an extremely complex hierarchy of sympathies, indifferences, and aversions of both the most short-lived and the most enduring kind. And in this complex, the sphere of indifference is relatively limited. For, our psychological activity responds to almost every impression that comes from another person with a certain determinate feeling. The subconscious, fleeting, changeful nature of this feeling only *seems* to reduce it to indifference. Actually, such indifference would be as unnatural to us as the vague character of innumerable contradictory stimuli would be unbearable. We are protected against both of these typical dangers of the city by antipathy, which is the preparatory phase of concrete antagonism and which engenders the distances and aversions without which we could not lead the urban life at all. The extent and combination of antipathy, the rhythm of its appearance and disappearance, the forms in which it is satisfied, all these, along with the more literally unifying elements, produce the metropolitan form of life in its irresolvable totality; and what at first glance appears in it as dissociation, actually is one of its elementary forms of sociation.

HOMOGENEITY AND HETEROGENEITY IN SOCIAL RELATIONS

RELATIONS OF CONFLICT do not by themselves produce a social structure, but only in cooperation with unifying forces. Only both together constitute the group as a concrete, living unit. In this respect, conflict thus is hardly different from any other form of relation which sociology abstracts out of the complexity of actual life. Neither love nor the division of labor, neither the common attitude of two toward a third nor friendship, neither party affiliation nor superordination of subordination is likely by itself alone to produce or permanently sustain an actual group. Where this seems so nevertheless, the process which is given one name actually contains several distinguishable forms of relation. Human nature does not allow the individual to be tied to another by one thread alone, even though scientific analysis is not satisfied until it has determined the specific cohesive power of elementary units.

Yet perhaps this whole analytic activity is purely subjective in a higher and seemingly inverse sense of the word: perhaps the ties between individuals are indeed often quite homogeneous, but our mind cannot grasp their homogeneity. The very relations that are rich and live on many different contents are apt to make us most aware of this mysterious homogeneity; and what we have to do is to represent it as the co-efficiency of several cohesive forces which restrict and modify one another, resulting in the picture which objective reality attains by a much simpler and much more consistent route. Yet we cannot follow it with our mind even though we would.

Processes *within* the individual are, after all, of the same kind. At every moment they are so complex and contain such a multitude of variegated and contradictory oscillations that to designate them by any *one* of our psychological concepts is always imperfect and actually misleading. For, the moments of the individual life, too, are never connected by only one thread—this is the picture analytic thought constructs of the unity of the soul, which is inaccessible to it. Probably much of what we are forced to represent to ourselves as mixed feelings, as composites of many drives, as the competition of opposite sensations, is entirely self-consistent. But the calculating intellect often lacks a paradigm for this unity and thus must construe it as the result of several elements. When we are attracted and at the same time repelled by things; when nobler and baser character traits seem mixed in a given action; when our feeling for a particular person is composed of respect and friendship or of fatherly, motherly, and erotic impulses, or of ethical and aesthetic valuations—then certainly these phenomena in themselves, as real psychological processes, are often homogeneous. Only we cannot designate them directly. For this reason, by means of various analogies, antecedent motives, external consequences, we make them into a concert of several psychological elements.

If this is correctt, then apparently complex relations between several individuals, too, must actually often be unitary. For instance, the distance which characterizes the relation between two associated individuals may appear to us as the result of an affection, which ought to bring about much greater closeness between them, and of a repulsion, which ought to drive them completely apart; and in as much as the two feelings restrict one another, the outcome is the distance we observe. But this may be entirely erroneous. The inner disposition of the relation itself may be those particular distances; basically the relation, so to speak, has a certain temperature which does not emerge as the balance of two temperatures, one higher, the other lower. We often interpret the quantity of superiority and suggestion which exists between two persons as produced by the strength of one of them, which is at the same time diminished by a certain weakness. While such strength and weakness may in fact exist, their separateness often does not become manifest in the actually existing relation. On the contrary, the relation may be determined by the total nature of its elements, and we analyze its immediate character into those two factors only by hindsight.

Erotic relations offer the most frequent illustrations. How often do they not strike us as woven together of love and respect, or disrespect; of love and the felt harmony of the individuals and, at the same time, their consciousness of supplementing each other through opposite traits; of love and an urge to dominate or the need for dependence. But what the observer or the participant himself thus divides into two intermingling trends may in reality be only one. In the relation as it actually exists, the total personality of the one acts on that of the other. The reality of the relation does not depend on the reflection that if it did not exist, its participants would at least inspire each other with respect or sympathy (or their contraries). Any number of times we designate such relations as mixed feelings or mixed relations, because we construe the effects the qualities of one individual would have upon the other *if* these qualities exerted their influence *in isolation*—which is precisely what they do *not* do in the relation as it exists. Aside from all this, the "mixture" of feelings and relations, even where we are fully entitled to speak of it, always remains a problematic expression. It uses a dubious symbolism to transfer a process which is represented spatially into the very different realm of psychological conditions.

This, then, probably is often the situation in respect to the so-called mixture of converging and diverging currents within a group. That is, the structure may be *sui generis*, its motivation and form being wholly self-consistent, and only in order to be able to describe and understand it, do we put it together, *post factum*, out of two tendencies, one monistic, the other antagonistic. Or else, these two do in fact exist, but only, as it were, *before* the relation itself originated. In the relation itself, they have fused into an organic unity in which neither makes itself felt with its own, isolated power.

This fact should not lead us to overlook the numerous cases in which contradictory tendencies really co-exist in separation and can thus be recognized at any moment in the over-all situation. As a special form of historical development, relations sometimes show at an early stage undifferentiated unity of convergent and divergent forces which separate only later with full distinctness. At courts in Central Europe we find, up to the thirteenth century, permanent bodies of noblemen who constitute a kind of council to the prince and live as his guests; but at the same time, almost like an estate, they represent nobility and must guard its interests even *against* the prince. The interests in common with those of the king (whose administration these nobles often serve) and the oppositional vigilance of their own rights as an estate exist in these councils not only separately side by side but in intimate fusion; and it is most likely that the position was felt as self-consistent, no matter how incompatible its elements appear to us now. In the England of that period, the baronial parliament is hardly yet distinguished from an enlarged royal council. Loyalty and critical or partisan opposition are still contained in germ-like unity. In general, as long as the problem is the crystallization of institutions whose task it is to solve the increasingly complex and intricate problem of the equilibrium within the group, it often is not clear whether the cooperation of forces for the benefit of the whole takes the form of opposition, competition, and criticism, or of explicit unity and harmony. There thus exists an initial phase of undifferentiation which, seen from a later, differentiated phase, appears as logically contradictory, but which is thoroughly in line with the undeveloped stage of the organization.

Subjective or personal relations often develop in an inverse manner. For it is usually in early cultural periods that the decisiveness of amity or enmity is relatively great. Halfway, unclear relations between persons—relations which have their roots in a twilight condition of feeling whose outcome might be hatred almost as easily as love, or whose undifferentiated character is even sometimes betrayed by oscillation between the two—such relations are more often found in ripe and overripe than in youthful periods.

ANTAGONISM AS AN ELEMENT
IN SOCIATION

WHILE ANTAGONISM by itself does not produce sociation, it is a sociological element almost never absent in it. Its role can increase to infinity, that is, to the point of suppressing all convergent elements. In considering sociological phenomena, we thus find a hierarchy of relationships. This hierarchy can also be constructed from the viewpoint of ethical categories, although ethical categories are generally not very suitable points of departure for the convenient and complete isolation of sociological elements. The value-feelings with which we accompany the actions of individual wills fall into certain series. But the relation between these series, on the one hand, and constructs of forms of social relation according to objective-conceptual viewpoints, on the other, is completely fortuitous. Ethics conceived of as a kind of sociology is robbed of its deepest and finest content. This is the behavior of the individual soul in and to itself, which does not enter at all into its external relations: its religious movements, which exclusively serve its own salvation or damnation; its devotion to the objective values of knowledge, beauty, significance, which transcend all connections with other people. The intermingling of harmonious and hostile relations, however, presents a case where the sociological and the ethical series coincide. It begins with A's action for B's benefit, moves on to A's own benefit by means of B without benefiting B but also without damaging him, and finally becomes A's egoistic action at B's cost. In as much as all this is repeated by B, though hardly ever in the same way and in the same proportions, the innumerable mixtures of convergence and divergence in human relations emerge.

To be sure, there are conflicts which seem to exclude all

other elements—for instance, between the robber or thug and his victim. If such a fight simply aims at annihilation, it does approach the marginal case of assassination in which the admixture of unifying elements is almost zero. If, however, there is any consideration, any limit to violence, there already exists a socializing factor, even though only as the qualification of violence. Kant said that every war in which the belligerents do not impose some restrictions in the use of possible means upon one another, necessarily, if only for psychological reasons, becomes a war of extermination. For where the parties do not abstain at least from assassination, breach of word, and instigation to treason, they destroy that confidence in the thought of the enemy which alone permits the materialization of a peace treaty following the end of the war. It is almost inevitable that an element of commonness injects itstelf into the enmity once the stage of open violence yields to any other relationship, even though this new relation may contain a completely undiminished sum of animosity between the two parties. After conquering Italy in the sixth century, the Lombards imposed on the conquered a tribute of one-third on the ground yield, and they did so in such a fashion that every single individual among the conquerors depended upon the tribute paid him by particular individuals among the conquered. In this situation, the conquered's hatred of their oppressors may be as strong as it is during the war itself, if not stronger, and it may be countered no less intensely by the conquerors—either because the hatred against those who hate us is an instinctive protective measure, or because, as is well known, we usually hate those whom we have caused to suffer. Nevertheless, the situation had an element of community. The very circumstance which had engendered the animosity—the enforced participation of the Lombards in the enterprises of the natives—at the same time made for an undeniable convergence of interests. Divergence and harmony became inextricably interwoven, and the content of the animosity actually developed into the germ of future commonness.

This formal type of relationship is most widely realized in the enslavement—instead of the extermination—of the imprisoned enemy. Even though slavery very often represents the extreme of absolute inner hostility, its occasion nevertheless produces a sociological condition and thus, quite frequently, its own attenuation. The sharpening of contrasts may be provoked directly for the sake of its own diminution, and by no means only as a violent measure, in the expectation that the antagonism, once it reaches a certain limit, will end because of exhaustion or the realization of its futility. It may also happen for the reason which sometimes makes monarchies give their own opposition princes as leaders— as did, for instance, Gustavus Vasa. To be sure, opposition is strengthened by this policy; elements which would otherwise stay away from it are brought to it by the new equilibrium; but at the same time, opposition is thus kept within certain limits. In apparently strengthening it on purpose, government actually blunts it by this conciliating measure.

Another borderline case appears to be the fight engendered exclusively by the lust to fight. If the conflict is caused by an object, by the will to have or control something, by rage or revenge, such a desired object or state of affairs make for conditions which subject the fight to norms or restrictions applying to both warring parties. Moreover, since the fight is centered in a purpose outside itself, it is qualified by the fact that, in principle, every end can be attained by more than one means. The desire for possession or subjugation, even for the annihilation of the enemy, can be satisfied through combinations and events other than fight. Where conflict is merely a means determined by a superior purpose, there is no reason not to restrict or even avoid it, provided it can be replaced by other measures which have the same promise of success. Where, on the other hand, it is exclusively determined by subjective feelings, where there are inner energies which *can* be satisfied only through fight, its substitution by other means is impossible; it is its own purpose and content and hence wholly free from the admixture of other forms of relation. Such a fight for its own sake seems to be suggested by a certain formal hostility drive which sometimes urges itself upon psychological observation. Its different forms must now be discussed.

THE PRIMARY NATURE OF HOSTILITY

SKEPTICAL MORALISTS speak of natural enmity between men. For them, *homo homini lupus* [man is wolf to man], and "in the misfortune of our best friends there is something which does not wholly displease us." But even the diametrically opposed moral philosophy, which derives ethical selflessness from the transcendental foundations of our nature, does not thereby move very far from the same pessimism. For after all, it admits that devotion to the Thou cannot be found in the experience and observation of our will. Empirically, rationally, man is pure egoist, and any deflection of this natural fact can occur in us, not through nature, but only through the *deux ex machina* of a metaphysical being. Hence natural hostility as a form or basis of human relations appears at least side by side with their other basis, sympathy. The strange lively interest, for instance, which people usually show in the suffering of others, can only be explained on the basis of a mixture of the two motivations. This deep-lying antipathy is also suggested by the phenomenon, not at all rare, of the "spirit of contradiction" (*Widerspruchsgeist*). It is found not only in those nay-sayers-on-principle who are the despair of their surroundings among friends, in families, in committees, and in the theatre public. Nor does this spirit celebrate its most characteristic triumphs in the realm of politics, in those men of opposition whose classical type Macaulay has described in the person of Robert Ferguson:

"His hostility was not to Popery or to Protestantitsm, to monarchical government or to republican government, to the house of Stuarts or to the house of Nassau, but to whatever was at the time established." All these cases which are usually considered to be types of "pure opposition" do not *necessarily* have to be such: ordinarily, the opponents conceive of themselves as defenders of threatened rights, as fighters for what is objectively correct, as knightly protectors of the minority.

It appears to me that much less striking phenomena reveal more clearly an abstract impulse to opposition—especially the quiet, often hardly known, fleeting temptation to contradict an assertion or demand, particularly a categorical one. This instinct of opposition emerges with the inevitability of a reflex movement, even in quite harmonious relationships, in very conciliatory persons. It mixes itself into the over-all situation even though without much effect. One might be tempted to call this a protective instinct—just as certain animals, merely upon being touched, automatically use their protective and aggressive apparatus. But this would precisely prove the primary, basic character of opposition. It would mean that the individual, even where he is not attacked but only finds himself confronted by purely objective manifestations of other individuals, cannot maintain himself except by means of opposition. It would mean that the first instinct with which the individual affirms himself is the negation of the other.

It seems impossible to deny an *a priori* fighting instinct, especially if one keeps in mind the incredibly picayunish, even silly, occasions of the most serious conflicts. An English historian reports that not long ago two Irish parties, whose enmity developed from a quarrel over the color of a cow, fought each other furiously throughout the whole country. Some decades ago, grave rebellions occurred in India as the consequence of a feud between two parties which knew nothing about one another except that they were, respectively, the party of the right hand and the party of the left. And this triviality of the causes of conflicts is paralleled by the childish behavior in which conflicts often end. In India, Mohammedans and Hindus live in a constant latent enmity which they document by the Mohammedans buttoning their outer garments to the right, and the Hindus to the left; by the Mohammedans, at common meals, sitting in a circle, and the Hindus in a row; by the poor Mohammedans using one side of a certain leaf for a plate, and the Hindus the other. In human hostility, cause and effect are often so heterogeneous and disproportionate that it is hard to determine whether the alleged issue really is the cause of the conflict or merely the consequence of long-existing opposition. The impossibility of ascertaining any rational basis of the hostility presents us with this uncertainty in regard to many details of the conflicts between the Roman and Greek circus parties, between the Homoousians and the Homoiousians, and of the Wars of the Roses and of the Guelfs and Ghibellines. The general impression is that human beings never love one another because of such picayunish trivia as lead them to violent hatred.

THE SUGGESTIBILITY OF HOSTILITY

THERE IS FINALLY another phenomenon which seems to me to point to a wholly primary need for hostility. This is the uncanny ease with which hostility can be suggested. It is usually much easier for the average person to inspire another individual with distrust and suspicion toward a third, previously indifferent person than with confidence and sympathy. It is significant that this difference is particularly striking in respect to these favorable or unfavorable moods and prejudices if they are at their beginning or have developed only to a slight degree. For, higher degrees, which lead to practical application, are not decided by such fleeting leanings (which, however, betray the fundamental instinct) but by more conscious considerations. The same fundamental fact is shown in merely another version, as it were, by the circumstance that quite indifferent persons may successfully suggest those slight prejudices which fly over the image of another like shadows, whereas only an authoritative or emotionally close individual succeeds in causing us to have the corresponding *favorable* prejudice.

Without this ease or irresponsibility with which the average person reacts to suggestions of an unfavorable kind, the *aliquid haeret* [social, emotional inertia] would perhaps not be so tragically true. The observation of certain antipathies, factions, intrigues, and open fights might indeed lead one to consider hostility among those primary human energies which are not provoked by the external reality of their objects but which create their own objects out of themselves. Thus it has been said that man does not have religion because he believes in God but that he believes in God because he has religion, which is a mood of his soul. In general, it is probably recognized that love, especially in youth, is not a mere reaction evoked by its object (as a color sensation is evoked in our optical apparatus), but that on the contrary, we have a need for loving and ourselves seize upon some object which satisfies this need—sometimes bestowing on it those characteristics which, we alleged, have evoked our love in the first place.

THE HOSTILITY DRIVE AND
ITS LIMITED POWER

THERE IS NOTHING to suggest that all this does not also hold of the development of the opposite emotion (except for a qualification, of which presently). There is nothing to suggest that the soul does not also have an inborn need for *hating* and *fighting,* and that often this need alone injects into the objects it takes for itself their hate-provoking qualities. This interpretation of hatred is not so obvious as is that of love. The reason probably is that the need for love, with its tremendous physiological pointedness in youth, is so palpably spontaneous, that is, so palpably determined by the actor (lover) rather than by the beloved, that, by comparison, the hate drive is only seldom found in stages of comparable acuteness which would make us equally conscious of its subjective, spontaneous character.[5]

Assuming that there indeed exists a formal hostility drive as the counterpart of the need for sympathy, it seems to me that historically it stems from one of those processes of distillation by which intra-individual movements leave an independent impulse as the residue of the forms which are common to them. All kinds of interests so often lead to conflicts over particular objects or to opposition against particular persons that, possibly as a residue of these conflicting interests, a general state of irritation, which by itself presses for manifestations of antagonism, has become part of the hereditary inventory of our species. It is well known that (for reasons often discussed) the mutual relation of primitive groups is almost always one of hostility. Perhaps the most decisive example comes from the American Indians, among whom every tribe was on principle considered in a state of war with every other tribe with which it had not concluded an explicit peace treaty. It must not be forgotten, however,

---

5. Fundamentally, all relations to others are distinguished according to the following questions (even though with innumerable answers ranging from the clear-cut affirmative to the clear-cut negative): (1) Is the psychological basis of the relation a drive (of the subject) which would develop even without external stimulus and on its own seeks an adequate object, either *finding* it in adequate form or making it so through imagination and necessity? Or (2) does the psychological basis of the relation consist in the response evoked by the nature or action of another person—whereby this response, too, of course, presupposes the *possibility* of being evoked; but this possibility would have remained latent without the stimulus and would not by itself have developed into a need. Intellectual and aesthetic, sympathetic and antipathetic relations are subject to this contrast from which alone they draw the forms of their development, intensity, and changes.

that in early stages of culture, war is almost the only form in which contact with alien groups is brought about at all. As long as inter-territorial commerce remains undeveloped, individual travel is something unknown, and intellectual communities do not transcend the boundaries of the group, war is the only sociological relation between different peoples. At such a stage, relations of the group *members* with one another have forms which are diametrically opposed to the interrelations among the *groups*. *Within* the closed circle, hostility usually means the termination of relations, withdrawal, or avoidance of contact, and these negative characteristics even accompany the passionate interaction of open fight. By contrast, these groups, as whole units, live in mutual indifference side by side as long as there is peace, while they gain active reciprocal significance for one another only in war. For this reason, the same drive to expand and to act, which *within* the group requires unconditional peace for the integration of interests and for unfettered interaction, may appear to the outside as a tendency toward war.

No matter how much psychological autonomy one may be willing to grant the antagonistic drive, this autonomy is not enough to account for all phenomena involving hostility. For in the first place, even the most spontaneous drive is restricted in its independence in as much as it does not apply to *all* objects but only to those which somehow appeal to it. Although hunger certainly originates in the subject without first being actualized by the object, it nevertheless does not seize on stones and wood but only on what is edible. Similarly, love and hate, too, however little their drives may derive from external stimuli, nevertheless seem to need some appealing structure of their objects with whose cooperation alone they yield the total phenomena that go by their names.

On the other hand, it seems probable to me that on the whole, because of its formal character, the hostility drive merely adds itself as a reinforcement (like the pedal on the piano, as it were) to controversies which are due to concrete causes. And where a conflict springs from the purely formal lust to fight—that is, from something entirely impersonal, fundamentally indifferent toward any content, even toward the adversary—even there, hatred and rage against the enemy as a person, and if possible interest in a prize for victory, inevitably grow in the course of the conflict because such emotions feed and increase its psychological strength. It is *expedient* to hate the adversary with whom one fights (for any reason), just as it is expedient to love a person whom one is tied to and has to get along with. The truth expressed by a popular Berlin song, "What one does out of love goes twice as well" ("*Was man aus Liebe tut, Das geht noch mal so gut*"), also goes for what one does out of hatred. The mutual behavior between people can only be understood by appreciating the inner adaptation which trains in us feelings most suitable to a given situation, whether they are to exploit or assert this situation, or are to bear or end it. By means of psychological connections, these feelings produce the forces which are necessary to execute the given task and to paralyze inner countercurrents. Hence no serious conflict probably lasts any length of time without being sustained by a *complex* of psychological impulses, even though this complex grows only gradually. This is of great sociological significance: the purity of conflict for the sake of conflict thus is seen to become interspersed partly with more objective interests, partly with impulses which can be satisfied by other means than fight, and which in practice form the bridge between conflict and other forms of interaction.

ANTAGONISTIC GAMES

I REALLY KNOW only a single case in which the fascination of fight and victory itself—elsewhere only an *element* in the antagonisms over particular contents—is the exclusive motivation: this is the antagonistic game (*Kampfspiel*), more precisely, the game which is carried on without any prize for victory (since the prize would lie outside of it). The purely sociological attraction of becoming master over the adversary, of asserting oneself against him, is combined here, in the case of games of skill, with the purely individual enjoyment of the most appropriate and successful movement; and in the case of games of luck, with favor by fate which blesses us with a mystical, harmonious relation to powers beyond the realm of the individual and social. At any rate, in its *sociological motivation*, the antagonistic game contains absolutely nothing except fight itself. The worthless chip which is often contested as passionately as is a gold piece, suggests the formal nature of this impulse, which even in the quarrel over gold often greatly exceeds any material interest.

But there is something else most remarkable: the realization of precisely this complete dualism presupposes sociological forms in the stricter sense of the word, namely, unification. One *unites* in order to fight, and one fights under the mutually recognized control of norms and rules. To repeat, these unifications do not enter into the *motivation* of the undertaking, even though it is through them that it takes shape. They rather are the technique without which such a conflict that excludes all heterogeneous or objective justifications could not materialize. What is more, the norms of the antagonistic game often are rigorous and impersonal and are observed on both sides with the severity of a code of honor—to an extent hardly shown by groups which are formed for cooperative purposes.

LEGAL CONFLICT   881274

THE PRINCIPLES of conflict and of unification, which holds the contrasts together in one whole, are shown in this example with the purity of almost an abstract concept. It thus reveals how each principle attains its full sociological meaning and effect only through the other. The same form which dominates the antagonistic game also governs legal conflict, even though not with the same neatness and separateness of the two factors involved. For legal conflict has an *object,* and the struggle can be satisfactorily terminated through the voluntary concession of that object. This does not occur in fights for the lust of fighting. In most cases, what is called the lust and passion of legal quarrels, is probably something quite different, namely, a strong feeling of justice or the impossibility of bearing an actual or alleged interference with the sphere of law with which the ego feels identified. All the uncompromising stubbornness and obstinacy with which parties at a trial so often bleed themselves to death has, even on the defendant's part, hardly the character of an offensive but, in a deeper sense, that of a defensive, since the question is the self-preservation of the person. This self-preservation is so inseparable from the person's possessions and rights that any inroad on them destroys it. It is only consistent to fight with the power of one's whole existence. Hence it probably is this individualistic drive, rather than the sociological drive to fight, which determines such cases.

In respect to the *form* of conflict, however, legal quarrel is indeed absolute. That is, on both sides the claims are put through with pure objectivity and with all means that are permitted; the conflict is not deflected or attenuated by any personal or in any other sense extraneous circumstances. Legal conflict is pure conflict in as much as nothing enters its whole action which does not belong to the conflict *as such* and serves its purpose. Elsewhere, even in the wildest struggles, something subjective, or some mere turn of fate, or some interference by a third party is at least possible. In legal conflict, all this is excluded by the objectivity with which only the fight and absolutely nothing else proceeds.

This elimination of all that is not conflict can of course lead to a formalism which becomes independent of all contents. On the one hand, we here have legal pettifoggery. In legal pettifoggery, it is not objective points which are weighed against one another; instead, concepts lead an entirely abstract fight. On the other hand, the conflict is sometimes delegated to agents which have no relation to what their contest is to decide. The fact that in higher cultures, legal quarrels are carried out by professional counsels, certainly serves the clean separation of the controversy from all personal associations which have nothing to do with it. But if Otto the Great decrees that a legal question must be decided through ordeal by combat, only the mere form—the occurrence of fighting and winning itself—is salvaged from the whole conflict of interests; only the form is the element common to the fight to be decided and to the individuals who decide it.

This case expresses in exaggeration or caricature the reduction and restriction of legal conflict to the mere element of fight itself. It is the most merciless type of contestation because it lies wholly outside the subjective contrast between charity and cruelty. But precisely because of its pure objectivity, it is grounded entirely in the premise of the unity and commonness of the parties—and this to a degree of severity and thoroughness hardly required by any other situation. Legal conflict rests on a broad basis of unities and agreements between the enemies. The reason is that both parties are equally subordinated to the law; they mutually recognize that the decision is to be made only according to the objective weight of their claims; they observe the forms which are unbreakably valid for both; and they are conscious that they are surrounded in their whole enterprise by a social power which alone gives meaning and certainty to their undertaking. The parties to a negotiation or a commercial affair form a unity in the same manner, even though to a less extent, for they recognize norms binding and obligatory to both, irrespective of the opposition of their interests. The *common* premises which exclude everything personal from legal conflict have that character of pure objectivity to which (on the other hand) correspond the inexorability and the acute and unconditional character of the conflict itself. Legal conflict thus shows the interaction between the dualism and the unity of sociological relations no less than antagonistic games do. The extreme and unconditional nature of conflict comes to the fore in the very meduim and on the very basis of the strict unity of common norms and conditions.

CONFLICTS OVER CAUSES

THIS SAME PHENOMENON is characteristic, finally, of all conflicts in which both parties have objective interests. In this case, the conflicting interests, and hence the conflict itself, are differentiated from the personalities involved. Here two things are possible. The conflict may focus on purely objective decisions and leave all personal elements outside itself and in a state of peace. Or on the contrary, it may involve precisely the persons in their subjective aspects without, however, thereby leading to any alteration or disharmony of the co-existing objective interests common to the two parties. The second type is characterized by Leibnitz's saying that he would run even after a deadly enemy if he could learn something from him. Such an attitude can obviously soften and attenuate the hostility itself; but its possible opposite result must also be noted. Hostility which goes along with solidarity and understanding in objective matters is indeed, so to speak, clean and certain in its justification. The consciousness of such a differentiation assures us that we do not harbor personal antipathy where it does not belong. But the good conscience bought with this discrimination may under certain circumstances lead to the very intensification of hostility. For where hostility is thus restricted to its real center, which at the same time is the most subjective layer of personality, we sometimes abandon ourselves to it more extensively, passionately, and with more concentration than when the hostile impulse carries with it a ballast of secondary animosities in areas which actually are merely infected by that center.

In the case in which the same differentiation inversely limits the conflict to impersonal interests, there too are two possibilities. On the one hand, there may be the elimination of useless embitterments and intensifications which are the price we pay for personalizing objective controversies. On the other hand, however, the parties' consciousness of being mere representatives of supra-individual claims, of fighting not for themselves but only for a cause, can give the conflict a radicalism and mercilessness which find their analogy in the general behavior of certain very selfless and very idealistically inclined persons. Because they have no consideration for themselves, they have none for others either; they are convinced that they are entitled to make anybody a victim of the idea for which they sacrifice themselves. Such a conflict which is fought out with the strength of the whole person while the victory benefits the cause alone, has a noble character. For, the noble individual is wholly personal but knows nevertheless how to hold his personality in reserve. This is why objectivity strikes us as noble. But once this differentiation has been achieved and the conflict thus objectified, it is, quite consistently, not subjected to a second restriction, which in fact would be a violation of the objective interest to which the fight has been limited. On the basis of this mutual agreement of the two parties, according to which each of them defends only his claims and his cause, renouncing all personal or egoistic considerations, the conflict is fought with unattenuated sharpness, following its own intrinsic logic, and being neither intensified nor moderated by subjective factors.

The contrast between unity and antagonism is perhaps most visible where both parties really pursue an identical aim—such as the exploration of a scientific truth. Here any yielding, any polite renunciation of the merciless exposure of the adversary, any peace prior to the wholly decisive victory would be treason against that objectivity for the sake of which the personal character has been eliminated from the fight. Ever since Marx, the social struggle has developed into this form, despite infinite differences in other respects. Since it has been recognized that the condition of labor is determined by the objective conditions and forms of production, irrespective of the desires and capacities of particular individuals, the personal bitterness of both general and local battles has greatly decreased. The entrepreneur is no longer a bloodsucker and damnable egoist, nor does the worker suffer from sinful greediness under all circumstances. Both parties have at least begun no longer to burden each other's consciences with their mutual demands and tactics as acts of personal meanness. In Germany, this objectification was started more nearly by means of theory, in as much as the personal and individualistic nature of antagonism was overcome by the more abstract and general character of the historical and class movement. In England, it was launched by the trade unions and was furthered by the rigorously supra-individual unity of their actions and those of the corresponding federations of entrepreneurs. The violence of the fight, however, has not decreased for that. On the contrary, it has become more pointed, concentrated, and at the same time more comprehensive, owing to the consciousness of the individual involved that he fights not only for himself, and often not for himself at all, but for a great super-personal aim.

An interesting example of this correlation is the workers' boycott of the Berlin breweries in 1894. This was one of the most violent local fights in recent decades,[6] carried out with the utmost force by both sides, but without any personal hatred of the brewers by the leaders of the boycott, or of

6. Written, presumably, shortly after 1900. Cf. *The Sociology of Georg Simmel, loc. cit.,* pp. lviii, (8), and lxii, IV.—Tr.

the workers by the business leaders. In fact, in the middle of the fight, two leaders of the two parties published their opinions of the struggle in the same periodical, both being objective in their presentations of the facts and hence agreeing on them, but differing, in line with their respective parties, on the practical consequences that were to be drawn from the facts. It thus appears that conflict can exclude all subjective or personal factors, thus quantitatively reducing hostility, engendering mutual respect, and producing understanding on all personal matters, as well as the recognition of the fact that both parties are driven on by historical necessities. At the same time, we see that this common basis increases, rather than decreases, the intensity, irreconcilability, and stubborn consistency of the fight.

The objective common to the conflicting parties on which alone their fight is based, can show itself in a much less noble manner than in the cases just discussed. This is true when the common feature is not an objective norm, an interest that lies above the egoism of the fighting parties, but their secret understanding in respect to an egoistic purpose which they both share. To a certain extent this was true of the two great English political parties in the eighteenth century. There was no basic opposition of political convictions between them, since the problem of both equally was the maintenance of the aristocratic regime. The strange fact was that two parties which between themselves completely dominated the area of political struggle, nevertheless did not fight each other radically—because they had a silent mutual pact against something which was not a political party at all. Historians have connected the parliamentary corruptibility of that period with this strange limitation of the fight. Nobody thought too badly of a party's selling its conviction in favor of the opposing party because the conviction of that opposing party had a rather broad, even though hidden common basis, and the fight lay elsewhere. The ease of corruption showed that here the restriction of the antagonism through a common feature did not make the conflict more fundamental and objective. On the contrary, it blurred it and contaminated its meaning as necessarily determined by objective circumstances.

In other, purer cases, when unity is the point of departure and the basis of the relationship, and conflict arises over this unity, the synthesis between the monism and antagonism of the relation can have the opposite result. A conflict of this sort is usually more passionate and radical than when it does not meet with a prior or simultaneous mutual belongingness to the parties. While ancient Jewish law permitted bigamy, it forbade marriage with two sisters (even though after the death of one her husband could marry the other), for this would have been especially apt to arouse jealousy. In other words, this law simply assumes as a fact of experience that antagonism on the basis of a common kinship tie is stronger than among strangers. The mutual hatred of very small neighboring states whose whole outlooks, local relations, and interests are inevitably very similar and frequently even coincide, often is much more passionate and irreconcilable than between great nations, which both spatially and objectively are complete strangers to one another. This was the fate of Greece and of post-Roman Italy, and a more intensive degree of it shook England after the Norman Conquest before the two races fused. These two lived scattered among one another in the same territory, were mutually bound by constantly operating vital interests, and were held together by one national idea—and yet intimately, they were complete mutual strangers, were, in line with their whole character, without reciprocal understanding, and were absolutely hostile to one another in regard to their power interests. Their reciprocal hatred, as has rightly been said, was more bitter than it can ever be between externally and internally separate groups.

Some of the strongest examples of such hatred are church relations. Because of dogmatic fixation, the minutest divergence here at once comes to have logical irreconcilability— if there is deviation at all, it is conceptually irrelevant whether it be large or small. A case in point are the confessional controversies between Lutherans and Reformed, especially in the seventeenth century. Hardly had the great separation from Catholicism occurred, when the whole, over the most trivial matters, split into parties which frequently said about one another that one could more easily make peace with the Popists than with the members of the other Protestant group. And in 1875 in Berne, when there was some difficulty over the place where Catholic services were to be held, the Pope did not allow them to be performed in the church used by the Old-Catholics, but in a Reformed church.

COMMON QUALITIES VS. COMMON MEMBERSHIP IN A LARGER SOCIAL STRUCTURE AS BASES OF CONFLICT

TWO KINDS of commonness may be the bases of particularly intense antagonisms: the common qualities and the common membership in a larger social structure. The first case goes back simply to the fact that we are discriminating beings (*Unterschiedswesen*). A hostility must excite consciousness the more deeply and violently, the greater the parties' similarity against the background of which the hostility rises. Where attitudes are friendly or loving, this is an excellent protective measure of the group, comparable to the warning function of pain in the organism. For it is precisely the keen awareness of dissonance against the prevailing general harmony which at once warns the parties to remove the grounds of conflict lest conflict half-consciously creep on and endanger the basis of the relation itself. But where this fundamental intention to get along under all circumstances is lacking, the consciousness of antagonism, sensitized as this consciousness is by similarity in other respects, will sharpen the antagonism itself. People who have many common features often do one another worse or "wronger" wrong than complete strangers do. Sometimes they do this because the large area common to them has become a matter of course, and hence what is temporarily different, rather than what is common, determines their mutual positions. Mainly, however, they do it because there is only little that is different between them; hence even the slightest antagonism has a relative significance quite other than that between strangers, who count with all kinds of mutual differences to begin with. Hence the family conflicts over which people profoundly in agreement sometimes break up. That they do so does by no means always prove that the harmonizing forces had weakened before. On the contrary, the break can result from so great a similarity of characteristics, leanings, and convictions that the divergence over a very insignificant point makes itself felt in its sharp contrast as something utterly unbearable.

We confront the stranger, with whom we share neither characteristics nor broader interests, objectively; we hold our personalities in reserve; and thus a particular difference does not involve us in our totalities. On the other hand, we meet the person who is very different from us only on certain points within a particular contact or within a coincidence of particular interests, and hence the spread of the conflict is limited to those points only. The more we have in common with another *as whole persons*, however, the more easily will our totality be involved in every single relation to him. Hence the wholly disproportionate violence to which normally well-controlled people can be moved within their relations to those closest to them. The whole happiness and depth of the relation to another person with whom, so to speak, we feel identical, lies in the fact that not a single contact, not a single word, not a single common activity or pain remains isolated but always clothes the whole soul which completely gives itself in it and is received in it. Therefore, if a quarrel arises between persons in such an intimate relationship, it is often so passionately expansive and suggests the schema of the fatal "Not you" (*"Du-überhaupt"*). Persons tied to one another in this fashion are accustomed to invest every direction in which they may turn with the totality of their being and feeling. Hence they also give conflicting accents and, as it were, a periphery by virtue of which it far outgrows its occasion and the objective significance of that occasion, and drags the total personalities into it.

CONFLICT IN INTIMATE RELATIONS

AT THE HIGHEST LEVEL of spiritual cultivation it is possible to avoid this, for it is characteristic of this level to combine complete mutual devotion with complete mutual differentiation. Whereas undifferentiated passion involves the totality of the individual in the excitement of a part or an element of it, the cultivated person allows no such part or element to transcend its proper, clearly circumscribed domain. Cultivation thus gives relations between harmonious persons the advantage that they become aware, precisely on the occasion of conflict, of its trifling nature in comparison with the magnitude of the forces that unify them.

Furthermore, the refined discriminatory sense, especially of deeply sensitive persons, makes attractions and antipathies more passionate if these feelings contrast with those of the past. This is true in the case of unique, irrevocable decisions concerning a given relationship, and it must be sharply distinguished from the everyday vacillations within a mutual belongingness which is felt, on the whole, to be unquestionable. Sometimes between men and women a fundamental aversion, even a feeling of hatred—not in regard to certain particulars, but the reciprocal repulsion of the total person—is the first stage of a relation whose second phase is passionate love. One might entertain the paradoxical suspicion that when indi-

viduals are destined to the closest mutual emotional relationship, the emergence of the intimate phase is guided by an
instinctive pragmatism so that the eventual feeling attains its
most passionate intensification and awareness of what it has
achieved by means of an opposite prelude—a step back before
running, as it were.

The inverse phenomenon shows the same form: the deepest hatred grows out of broken love. Here, however, not
only the sense of discrimination is probably decisive but
also the denial of one's own past—a denial involved in such
change of feeling. To have to recognize that a deep love—
and not only a sexual love—was an error, a failure of intuition
(*Instinkt*), so compromises us before ourselves, so splits the
security and unity of our self-conception, that we unavoid-
ably make the object of this intolerable feeling pay for it.
We cover our secret awareness of our own responsibility for
it by hatred which makes it easy for us to pass all responsibility on to the other.

This particular bitterness which characterizes conflicts
within relationships whose nature would seem to entail harmony is a sort of positive intensification of the platitude
that relations show their closeness and strength in the absence
of differences. But this platitude is by no means true without
exception. That very intimate groups, such as marital couples,
which dominate, or at least touch on, the whole content of
life, should contain no occasions for conflict is quite out of
the question. It is by no means the sign of the most genuine
and deep affection never to yield to those occasions but
instead to prevent them in far-ranging anticipation and to
cut them short immediately by mutual yielding. On the contrary, this behavior often characterizes attitudes which though
affectionate, moral, and loyal, nevertheless lack the ultimate,
unconditional emotional devotion. Conscious of this lack,
the individual is all the more anxious to keep the relation free
from any shadow and to compensate his partner for that lack

through the utmost friendliness, self-control, and consideration. But another function of this behavior is to soothe one's
own consciousness in regard to its more or less evident un-
truthfulness which even the most sincere or even the most
passionate will cannot change into truthfulness—because feelings are involved which are not accessible to the will but,
like fate itself, exist or do not exist.

 The felt insecurity concerning the basis of such relations
often moves us, who desire to maintain the relation at all
cost, to acts of exaggerated selflessness, to the almost mechanical insurance of the relationship through the avoidance, on
principle, of every possibility of conflict. Where on the
other hand we are certain of the irrevocability and unre-
servedness of our feeling, such peace at any price is not
necessary. We know that no crisis can penetrate to the
foundation of the relationship—we can always find the other
again on this foundation. The strongest love can stand a blow
most easily, and hence it does not even occur to it, as is
characteristic of a weaker one, to fear that the consequences
of such a blow cannot be faced, and it must therefore be
avoided by all means. Thus, although conflict among inti-
mates can have more tragic results than among less intimate
persons, in the light of the circumstances discussed, precisely
the most firmly grounded relation may take a chance at
discord, whereas good and moral but less deeply rooted relationships apparently follow a much more harmonious and
conflictless course.

This sociological sense of discrimination and the accentuation of conflict on the basis of similarity have a special nuance
in cases where the separation of originally homogeneous
elements occurs on purpose. Here separation does not follow
from conflict but, on the contrary, conflict from separation.
Typical of this is the way the renegade hates and is hated.
The recall of earlier agreement has such a strong effect
that the new contrast is infinitely sharper and bitterer than

if no relation at all had existed in the past. Moreover, often both parties realize the difference between the new phase and the similarity remembered (and the unambiguousness of this difference is of the greatest importance to them) only by allowing it to grow far beyond its original locus and to characterize every point which is at all comparable. This aim of securing the two respective positions transforms theoretical or religious defection into the reciprocal charge of heresy in respect to all moral, personal, internal and external matters—a charge not necessarily ensuing where the same difference occurs between strangers. In fact, the degeneration of a difference in *convictions* into hatred and fight ordinarily occurs only when there were essential, original similarities between the parties. The (sociologically very significant) "respect for the enemy" is usually absent where the hostility has arisen on the basis of previous solidarity. And where enough similarities continue to make confusions and blurred borderlines possible, points of difference need an emphasis not justified by the issue but only by that danger of confusion. This was involved, for instance, in the case of Catholicism in Berne, mentioned earlier. Roman Catholicism does not have to fear any threat to its identity from external contact with a church so different as the Reformed Church, but quite from something as closely akin as Old-Catholicism.

CONFLICT AS A THREAT TO THE GROUP

THIS EXAMPLE already touches upon the second type which is relevant here, although in practice it more or less coincides with the first. It is the case of hostility whose intensification is grounded in a feeling of belonging together, of unity, which by no means always means similarity. The reason for treating this type separately is that instead of the sense of discrimination, it shows a very different fundamental factor, namely, the peculiar phenomenon of social hatred. This hatred is directed against a member of the group, not from personal motives, but because the member represents a danger to the preservation of the group. In so far as intra-group conflict involves such a danger, the two conflicting parties hate each other not only on the concrete ground which produced the conflict but also on the sociological ground of hatred for the enemy of the group itself. Since this hatred is mutual and each accuses the other of responsibility for the threat to the whole, the antagonism sharpens—precisely because both parties to it belong to the same social unit.

Most characteristic here are the cases which do not lead to the proper break-up of the group. For once the group is dissolved, there is a certain release of the conflict; personal differences have been discharged sociologically; the thorn of ever new irritation has been removed. The tension between intra-group antagonism and group continuation must, on the contrary, lead to continued conflict. Just as it is terrible to be in conflict with a person to whom one is tied—externally or, in the most tragic cases, by an internal bond—but from whom one cannot tear oneself loose even if one wished to, so the bitterness is equally intensified when one does not *want* to leave the group because one feels this unit to be an objective value, a threat to which calls for fight and hatred. From this constellation springs the violence characteristic of conflicts within a political faction, a labor union, a family, etc.

Here, conflicts within the individual offer an analogy. In certain cases, they may be held down by the feeling that a struggle between sensuous and ascetic, egoistic and moral, practical and intellectual tendencies not only does injustice to one or both of these contrasting claims—not allowing full life to either of them—but menaces the very unity, equilibrium, and strength of the whole individual. Where on the contrary this feeling is not enough to check the conflict, it gives it a bitter and desperate accent—as if the fight were about something much more essential than the immediate issue in question. The energy with which each of the conflicting tendencies wishes to subjugate the other, feeds not only on its own egoistic interest, so to speak, but on the much more comprehensive interest in the maintenance of the ego which is torn apart and destroyed by the conflict, unless the conflict ends in unambiguous victory. Just so, conflict within a closely knit group often enough grows beyond the extent justified by its occasion and by the interest to the group immediately attendant on this occasion; for in addition, this conflict is associated with the feeling that the discord is not a matter only of the two parties but of the group as a whole. Each party fights, as it were, in the name of the whole group and must hate in its adversary not only its own enemy but at the same time the enemy of the higher sociological unit.

JEALOUSY

FINALLY, there is a fact by which the extreme violence of antagonistic excitement is linked to the closeness of belonging together. This fact, though apparently quite individual, actually is of great sociological significance. It is jealousy. Linguistic usage is ambiguous in regard to this concept; often it does not distinguish it from envy. Both affects are undoubtedly of the greatest importance for the shaping of human conditions. In both a value is at stake which a third party actually or symbolically prevents us from attaining or keeping. Where it is a matter of attaining, we shall here speak of envy; where of keeping, of jealousy. But the use of definitions is of course quite irrelevant as long as the psychological-sociological processes are clearly distinguished. It is characteristic of the jealous individual to have a rightful claim to possession, whereas envy refers to the desirability of what is denied it, not to the legitimacy of any claim. To the envious individual it is irrelevant whether the good is denied him because somebody else possesses it or whether even its loss or renunciation by that other individual would not let him obtain it. Jealousy, on the contrary, is determined in its inner direction and color precisely by the fact that we are prevented from possession because the possession is in somebody else's hands, and that if this were otherwise, we would become the possessors at once. The feeling of the envious individual turns more around possession, that of the jealous person more around the possessor. One can envy somebody's fame even though one has not the slightest claim to fame, but one is jealous of a famous man if one thinks that one deserves fame as much or more than he does. What is embittering and gnawing to the jealous individual is a certain fiction of feeling—no matter how unjustified or even nonsensical it may be—that the other has, so to speak, stolen the fame from him. Jealousy, whatever the exceptional psychological constellation from which it may have arisen, is a sensation of such a specific kind and power that it internally complements its typical situation.

Midway on the continuum between the phenomena of envy and jealousy thus described, there is a third one which may be designated as begrudging (*Missgunst*). "Begrudging" is the envious desire of an object, not because it is especially desirable but because the other has it. This kind of feeling may grow to either of two extremes, both of which end up by negating one's own possession. One form is that passionate begrudging which dispenses with the object or in fact destroys it, rather than leaving it in the hands of the other. The second form is complete indifference or even aversion toward the object, accompanied by the utter unbearability of the thought that the other possesses it. Such forms of begrudging are enmeshed in a thousand degrees and mixtures in the reciprocal behavior of human beings. They cover considerable portions of the large problem area in which people's relations to things are revealed as causes or effects of their relations to one another. For here it is not only the question of desiring money or power, affection or social position, through com-

peting with another person or through surpassing or eliminating him, whereby these activities are techniques, identical
in their inner meaning with conquering physical obstacles.
Rather, in these modifications of begrudging, the feeling which
accompanies such external and secondary relations among
persons develops into autonomous sociological forms in which
the desire for the object has become mere *content*. That this
is so can be seen in the fact that the interest in the objective
purpose has been slouched off or, rather, has been reduced to
the intrinsically irrelevant material around which the personal relation crystallizes.

This is the general basis on which emerges the significance
of jealousy for our problem, conflict. More particularly, this
is so when the content of jealousy is a person or the relation
of a given individual to that person. In fact, it seems to me
linguistic usage does not recognize jealousy in regard to a
purely impersonal object. What concerns us here is the
relation between a jealous individual and the person for
whose sake his jealousy is directed toward a third individual.
The relation to that third individual itself has a very different, sociologically much less specific and complicated, formal
character. For, the rage and hatred, contempt and cruelty
against *him* are built precisely on the premise of a *belonging
together*, of an external or internal, real or presumed claim
to love, friendship, recognition, union of some sort. Whether
felt on both sides or on one only, the antagonism is the more
intensive and extensive, the more unconditional the unity
from which it started and the more passionate the longing to
overcome it. The frequent, apparent vacillation of the jealous
person between love and hate means that these two layers
(of which the second covers the first in its whole expanse)
alternatively command his stronger awareness.

Here it is very important to remember the condition indicated earlier, namely, the *right* that the jealous individual
believes he has to the psychological or physical possession,

the love or the veneration of the person who is the object of his jealousy. A man may *envy* another's possession of a woman, but he is jealous only if he himself has some *claim* to possessing her. This claim may well consist exclusively in the mere passion of his desire, for it is a general human trait to derive a right from such a desire. The child excuses himself for taking something forbidden to him by saying that he "wanted it so much." At a duel, the adulterer, if he has the slightest trace of conscience, could not aim at the offended husband if he did not see in his own love for the other's wife a right to her, which he defends against the husband's merely legal right. Everywhere the mere fact of possession is considered the right to possession.

Just so, the stage preceding possession, namely, the desire for it, may grow into such a right. In fact, the double meaning of "claim"—simple desire and legally grounded desire—alludes to the fact that the will likes to increase the right of its strength by the strength of its right. To be sure, precisely because of this legal claim, jealousy often is the most pitiful spectacle; for to make *legal* claims to such feelings as love and friendship is to make an attempt with wholly inadequate means. The level on which one can operate on the basis of any right, external or internal, does not even touch the level on which these feelings lie. To wish to enforce them through a right, no matter how profound and well-acquired in other respects, is as senseless as if one wanted to order back to its cage a bird which has escaped from it beyond the reach of sight and hearing. This hopelessness of the right to love produces the phenomenon characteristic of jealousy, that is, the eventual hanging on to the *external proofs* of feeling, which can indeed be enforced by an appeal to duty. By means of this miserable satisfaction and self-deception, jealousy preserves the "body" of the relationship—and does as if it had caught in it something of its "soul."

The *claim* advanced by the jealous person is often fully

recognized by the other party. Like every right between persons, this claim means or produces a sort of unity. It is the ideal or legal content of a group, or a positive relationship of some sort, or at least their subjective anticipation. To this existing and continuing unity is added its simultaneous negation, and thus the situation ripe for jealousy is created. Contrary to other situations in which unity and antagonism interact, in the situation conducive to jealousy these two forces are not distributed among different areas, being held together and against one another only by the total personality. On the contrary, there is the denial of the very unity which still exists in some inner or outer form and is felt by at least one of the two parties so to exist, actually or ideally. The feeling of jealousy interjects a very peculiar, blinding, irreconcilable bitterness between two persons. For, the separation between them revolves precisely around the point of their *connection*, and the negative element in the tension between them thus attains the highest possible sharpness and accentuation.

The complete control of the inner situation by this formal-sociological constellation explains the strange, actually unlimited, range of motives upon which jealousy may feed. It also explains why its development is often incomprehensible as far as its content is concerned. Where either the very structure of the relation or the psychology of the individual is disposed toward such a synthesis of synthesis and antithesis, any occasion will develop the consequences—and these consequences, obviously, will be the more appealing, the more often they have been developed in the past. The jealous person can never see more than *one* interpretation. Thus, jealousy finds a completely malleable instrument in the fact that all human deeds and words admit of *several* interpretations of their intentions and attitudes. Jealousy can combine the most passionate hatred with the continuation of the most passionate love, and the lingering of the most intimate unity with the destruction of both parties—for, the jealous individual destroys the relation just as much as that relation invites him to destroy his partner. Thus, jealousy is perhaps that sociological phenomenon in which the building of antagonism upon unity attains its subjectively most radical form.

Chapter Two

Competition

PARTICULAR KINDS of such a synthesis are found in the phenomena lumped together under the name of competition. The foremost sociological characteristic of competition is the fact that conflict in it is indirect. In so far as one gets rid of an adversary or damages him directly, one does not compete with him. In general, linguistic usage reserves the term only for conflicts which consist in parallel efforts by both parties concerning the same prize. The difference of this from other kinds of conflict can perhaps be described in more detail as follows.

THE SUBJECTIVE GOAL VS.
THE OBJECTIVE RESULT OF COMPETITION

THE PURE FORM of the competitive struggle is above all not offensive and defensive, for the reason that the prize of the fight is not in the hands of either adversary. If one fights with somebody to obtain his money, wife, or fame, one uses quite other forms and techniques than if one *competes* with him as to who is to channel the public's money into his pockets, who is to win the woman's favor, who, by deed or word, is to make a greater name for himself. In many other kinds of conflict, victory over the adversary not only automatically secures, but itself is, the prize of victory. In competition, instead, there are two other combinations.

(1) Where victory over the competitor is the chronologically first necessity, it itself means nothing. The goal of the whole action is attained only with the availability of a value

which does not depend on that competitive fight at all. The businessman who succeeds in having his competitor suspected of unsoundness by the public gains nothing if the public's needs are suddenly deflected from his merchandise. The lover who eliminates or shames his rival is not a step ahead if the lady does not bestow her favors on him either. A religious denomination competing for a proselyte will not be chosen by him merely because it eliminates its competitor by proving its inadequacy—unless the proselyte's own needs can be satisfied by it. It is the specific coloration of the competitive struggle that its outcome itself does not constitute the goal, as it does wherever anger, revenge, or the ideal value of victory as such motivates a fight.

(2) The second type of competition perhaps differs even more greatly from other kinds of conflict. Here the struggle consists only in the fact that each competitor by himself aims at the goal, without using his strength on the adversary. This strange kind of fight is exemplified by the runner who only by his fastness, by the businessman who only by the price of his goods, by the proselytizer who only by the force of the inner conviction of his doctrine aims to reach his goal. This type of competition equals all other kinds of conflict in intensity and passionate effort. It is pushed to its utmost concentration by the reciprocal consciousness of the participants that each of them so concentrates. And yet, from a superficial standpoint, it proceeds as if there existed no adversary but only the aim.

This undeflected concentration on the aim permits competition to absorb contents over which the antagonism becomes purely formal. It then not only serves the common purpose of both parties but also allows the loser to benefit from the victory of the victor. In the Turkish siege of Malta in 1565, the grand master distributed the forts of the island among the various nations to which the knights belonged. Competition for the peak of bravery among the nations could thus be exploited for the defense of the whole, the island. This is genuine competition; but any damage to the competitor which might prevent the full application of his strength in the competitive struggle is excluded from the start. The Maltese example is so pure because the desire to win the honorable fight is assumed to elicit an extraordinary show of effort; and yet, victory can only be attained by the concomitance of benefit to the loser. Similarly, ambitious competition in the field of science aims not only at the adversary but at the *common* aim, on the assumption that the knowledge gained by the victor also is the gain and advantage of the loser. This special intensification of the principle is usually absent in artistic competition because, in view of the individualistic nature of art, the objective over-all value in which both parties equally participate is not apparent to them, although ideally perhaps it exists. The absence is even more obvious in business competition for the consumer; it too, however, is an illustration of the same formal principle. For even here, competition directly focuses upon the maximum result, and the net effect is the benefit of a third party or of all.

In this second form of competition, then, the subjectivity of the final goal and the objectivity of the final result interweave in the most fascinating manner. A super-individual, objective or social unit supersedes both parties and their fight. Each party fights its adversary without turning against him, without touching him, so to speak. The subjective, antagonistic mainspring thus leads to the realization of objective values, and victory in the fight is not really the success of the fight itself but, precisely, of the realization of values outside of it.

Here lies the immense value of competition for the social circle of which the competitors are members. The other types of conflict—where the prize is originally in the hands of one of the parties, or where an initial hostility, rather than the attainment of a prize, motivates the fight—make for the mutual annihilation of the combatants, and to society as a whole leave only the difference obtained by subtracting the weaker from the stronger force. Competition, on the other hand, in so far as it remains free from admixtures of these other forms, usually *increases* values through its incomparable sociological constellation. The reason is that from the standpoint of society, it offers subjective motives as the means of producing objective social values; and from the standpoint of the competing parties, it uses the production of objective values as means for attaining subjective satisfaction.[1]

---

1. This is a very pure case of the common type according to which what is an ultimate aim for the individual is a means for the species, the group, in short, for the encompassing social structure; and vice versa. This is true above all and in a large sense for man's relation to metaphysical totality, his God. In any idea of a divine world-plan, the individual's ultimate purposes are nothing but steps and means which help realize the absolute, ultimate end of all earthly movements, as posited in the divine spirit. Yet for the individual, in his unconditional interest in his ego, not only empirical reality but also that transcendental reality itself, is merely a means to his own purposes. He seeks the bliss of tranquil, redeemed perfection or ecstatic fullness in God, his well-being on earth or his salvation in the beyond, by means of God, who mediates it for him. As God, as absolute being, comes to Himself by way of man, so man comes to himself by way of God. This pattern had long been noted in respect to the relation between the individual and his species in the biological sense: erotic enjoyment, which for the individual is a self-justified, ultimate purpose, is for the species only a means whereby it secures its perpetuation beyond the moment. Inversely, this maintenance of the species, which is considered its purpose, at least by analogy, often enough is for the individual only the means of perpetuating himself in his children and of giving his property, his characteristics, his vitality a kind of immortality. What in social relations is called the harmony of interests between society and the individual amounts to the same thing. Individual activity is pre-designed and regulated by norms in order to carry on and develop the legal, moral, political, and cultural conditions of man; but on the whole, this is possible only because the individual's own eudamonistic, moral, material, and abstract interests appropriate these super-individual values as means. Thus, for instance, science is a content of objective culture and, as such, a self-sufficient, ultimate purpose of societal development; but for the individual, all extant science, including the portion he himself adds to it, is only a means for the satisfaction of his own cognitive drive. These relations certainly are not always of such a harmonious symmetry. Often enough they involve the

THE SOCIALIZING AND
CIVILIZING FUNCTION OF COMPETITION

YET THE PROGRESS of its content which competition achieves
by means of its peculiarly interwoven form of interaction[2]
is not so important here as is its immediately sociological
process. The aim for which competition occurs within a
society is presumably always the favor of one or more third
persons. Each of the competing parties therefore tries to
come as close to that third one as possible. Usually, the
poisonous, divisive, destructive effects of competition are
stressed, and for the rest it is merely admitted that it creates
certain values as its product. But in addition, it has, after
all, this immense sociating effect. Competition compels the
wooer who has a co-wooer, and often in this way alone
comes to be a wooer properly speaking, to go out to the
wooed, come close to him, establish ties with him, find
his strengths and weaknesses and adjust to them, find all
bridges, or cast new ones, which might connect the competitor's own being and doing with his.

To be sure, this often happens at the price of the competitor's own dignity and of the objective value of his product. Competition, above all competition among the makers of
the highest intellectual products, makes those who are destined to guide the mass subordinate themselves to it. In order
to permit the effective exercise of their function as teachers,

contradiction that, while both whole and part treat themselves as ultimate
purposes and the other, therefore, as means, neither of them is ready to
accept this role of mere means. Hence result frictions which can be felt at
every point of life and which permit the realization of the purposes of
whole and parts only with certain losses. The mutual exhaustion of forces,
which is not accompanied by an improvement of the positive result, and
the failure to reward and utilize the forces which turn out to be the weaker
ones, constitute such losses within competition, which otherwise so distinctly shows the symmetry of opposite teleological series.

2. "*Wechselwirkungsform.*" "*Wechselwirkung*" itself is translated as "interaction." On the term and its various renditions, see *The Sociology of
Georg Simmel, loc. cit.*, p. lxiv.—Tr.

party leaders, artists, or journalists, they must obey the instincts or moods of the mass once the mass can choose among them, which it can because of their competition. As far as *content* is concerned, this certainly makes for a reversal of the hierarchy of social life-values; but this does not detract from the *formal* significance of competition for the synthesis of society. Innumerable times, it achieves what usually only love can do: the divination of the innermost wishes of the other, even before he himself becomes aware of them. Antagonistic tension with his competitor sharpens the businessman's sensitivity to the tendencies of the public, even to the point of clairvoyance, in respect to future changes in the public's tastes, fashions, interests—not only the businessman's, but also the journalist's, artist's, bookseller's, parliamentarian's. Modern competition is described as the fight of all against all, but at the same time it is the fight of all *for* all. Nobody will deny the tragedy of social elements working against one another, instead of for; of the squandering of innumerable forces in the struggle against the competitor— forces which could be used for positive achievements; or, finally, of the discarding of the positive and valuable achievement, unused and unrewarded, as soon as a more valuable or at least a more appealing one competes with it.

But all these liabilities of competition in the social balance sheet must only be added to the immense synthetic force of the fact that, in society, competition is competition for man, a wrestling for applause and effort, exemption and devotion of all kinds, a wrestling of the few for the many, as well as of the many for the few. In short, it is a web of a thousand sociological threads by means of conscious concentration on the will and feeling and thinking of fellowmen, of the adaptation of the producers to the consumers, of the delicately multiplied possibilities of gaining favor and connection. Once the narrow and naïve solidarity of primitive social conditions yielded to decentralization (which was bound to have been the immediate result of the quantitative enlargement of the group), man's effort toward man, his adaptation to the other, seems possible only at the price of competition, that is, of the simultaneous fight *against* a fellowman *for* a third one—*against* whom, for that matter, he may well compete in some other relationship *for* the former. Given the breadth and individualization of society, many kinds of interest, which eventually hold the group together throughout its members, seem to come alive and stay alive only when the urgency and requirements of the competitive struggle force them upon the individual.

The socializing power of competition shows itself not only in these coarser, so-to-speak public, cases. We find two parties competing for a third in numberless combinations of family and love relationships, of social small talk and discussions over convictions, of friendship and satisfactions of one's vanity; sometimes, of course, only in allusions, beginnings which are dropped, side phenomena and partial phenomena of an over-all process. Wherever it occurs, however, the antagonism of the competitors if paralleled by some offering, coaxing, promising, imposing, which sets each of them in relation to the third party. For the victor in particular, this relation often attains an intensity which it would not have without the excitement by the chances of competition and without the peculiar, continuous comparison of his own achievement with the achievement of the other, which is possible only through competition. The more liberalism penetrates not only economic and political conditions but also those of the family, sociability, the church, friendship, stratification, and general social intercourse—that is, the less these conditions are pre-determined and regulated by broad, historical norms and the more they are left to shifting forces or to an unstable equilibrium which must be attained from case to case—the more will their shape depend on continual competitions. And the result of these competitions will in turn depend in most cases upon the interest, love, hope which the competitors know to arouse in different degrees in these or those third parties, the centers of the competitive movements.

Man's most valuable object is man, directly and indirectly. Indirectly, because in him are stored the energies of sub-human nature, as in the animal we eat or make work for us, are stored those of the vegetable kingdom; and in plants, those of sun and earth, air and water. Man is the most condensed, most fruitfully exploitable phenomenon; and the necessity of psychologically winning him over grows in the measure in which slavery, that is, his mechanical appropriation, weakens. The fight against man, which was a fight for him and his enslavement, thus changes into the more complex phenomenon of competition. To be sure, in it too, a man fights another man, but *for* a third one. And the winning over of that third one can be achieved in a thousand ways only through the sociological means of persuasion or conviction, surpassing or underselling, suggestion or threat, in short, through psychological connection. But just as often, this winning over also means in its effect such a psychological connection, the founding of a relationship—from the momentary relation established by a purchase in a store to marriage. As the intensity and condensation of life-contents increases culturally, the struggle for the most condensed of all goods, the human soul, must take on ever larger proportions and must multiply and deepen interactions which bring men together and which are both the means and the ends of that struggle.

ORGANIC SOLIDARITY VS. ISOLATION AS PROTECTIONS OF THE GROUP AGAINST INTRA-GROUP CONFLICT

THIS SUGGESTS already how groups are distinguished in their sociological character according to the extent and kind of competition they admit. Obviously, here is a problem of correlation, to which all of the discussion thus far has contributed: there is a relation between the structure of every social group and the measure of hostility it can afford among its members. For political society, the criminal code often indicates the limit beyond which quarrel, revenge, violence, and exploitation are no longer compatible with the maintenance of the group. The content of this code has therefore been characterized as the ethical minimum. But this is not quite correct. For a state would break apart if its members rigorously avoided all that is prohibited by the criminal law, while yet engaging in those attacks, damages, and hostilities which are possible under it. Every criminal code expects that most of these destructive energies are prevented from developing by inhibitions to which the code itself does not contribute. The minimum of ethical, peaceful behavior without which civil society could not exist thus goes beyond the categories guaranteed by the criminal code. On the basis of experience, it is assumed that these disturbances which are left unpunished do not by themselves exceed a socially bearable degree.

The more narrowly unified the group, the more can the hostility among its members have quite opposite consequences. On the one hand, the group, precisely because of its intimacy, can stand inner antagonisms without breaking apart, since the strength of the synthetic forces can cope with that of their antitheses. On the other hand, a group whose very principle is a considerable unity and feeling of belongingness is to this extent particularly threatened by every inner conflict. According to other circumstances, the same centripetality makes the group either more or less capable of resisting the dangers arising from animosities among its members.

Such close units as marriage show both at the same time. There probably is no other group which can stand such

insane hatred, such complete antipathy, such continual collisions and injuries without outwardly breaking apart. On
the other hand, though not the only relationship, marriage
is one of the few which through a hardly noticeable, hardly
verbalized split, even through a single antagonistic word,
can so lose the depth and beauty of its meaning that no passionate will of even both partners restores it.

Among larger groups, two apparently opposite structures
can afford considerable measures of hostility. One consists
of easily appealing relationships which effect a certain solidarity of their members by virtue of which damages resulting from hostile clashes here and there can be remedied with
relative ease. Here the members give the whole so much
strength or so many values that the whole can permit them
the freedom of antagonism since it can count on the expenditure of strength resulting from these antagonisms to be cov-
ered by other income, as it were. This is one reason why
well-organized groups can afford more inner splits and frictions than can more mechanical, internally disconnected con-
glomerations. The unity which can be brought about in a
larger group only through a more complex organization can
more easily balance the credits and debits within its social
life, and can bring any force available to bear on the points
of weakness that results from discords among its members
(or from other sources of loss). The very opposite social
structure has the same over-all effect: It is comparable to
the bottom of a ship which is composed of many watertight
compartments—if it is damaged, the water can still not penetrate all of it. Here the social principle is thus a certain
separation of the colliding parties. They must come to terms
with what they do to each other and must bear their damages
alone, without harming the existence of the whole.

There are thus two methods: organic solidarity, where
the whole makes up for damages from partial conflicts; and
isolation, where the whole preserves itself against such dam-

ages. The right choice between these two methods, or their right combination, is of course a vital question for every group, from the family to the state, from the economic to the spiritual union. At the one extreme is the modern state, which not only bears the struggles of its political parties despite the many forces which are dissipated in them, but even exploits these struggles to the advantage of its equilibrium and growth. At the opposite end is the ancient and medieval city state, which was often weakened by inner party conflicts to the point of annihilation. On the whole, the larger the group, the greater the possibility of its combining both methods. This is done in the sense that the parties themselves must settle the primary handicaps which result from their conflicts, while the secondary consequences of these conflicts for the life of the whole are met by the whole which brings its reserves into play. Evidently, this combination is difficult where the group is small and its members thus are closely connected.

COMPETITION WITHIN THE GROUP
AND THE STRUCTURE OF THE GROUP

I NOW COME BACK to the specific relation between the *competitive* struggle and the structure of the group in which it takes place. Above all, there is the distinction between two cases—where the very interests of the group necessitate a structure prohibiting or limiting competition; and where these interests, while accessible to competition, prevent it because of a particular historical circumstance or a general principle which supersedes them.

There are two conditions under which the first can occur. If there is competition for something not available or accessible to all competitors and accruing only to the winner among them, then competition, clearly, is impossible—either the members of the group do not strive after a good which is equally desirable to all of them, or they do, but the good is equally available to all. The first alternative is likely to obtain where sociation springs not from a common *terminus ad quem* but from a common *terminus a quo*,[3] from a common root—above all, in the family.

COMPETITION IN THE FAMILY

TO BE SURE, there may be occasional competition within a family. The children may compete for their parents' love or inheritance, or the parents for the love of their children. But such competition is determined by personal accident, as it is in the case of two brothers who are competitors in business. It bears no relation to the *principle* of the family, which is that of an organic life. The organism is its own purpose. It does not point beyond itself toward a goal which is external to it and for whose attainment its component parts compete. Certainly, purely personal hostility from natural antipathy is opposed to the principle of peace without which the family cannot exist in the long run. Yet the very intimacy of its common life, the social and economic interdependence, the somewhat violent presumption of its unity —all these give frictions, tensions, oppositions a strong chance to occur. In fact, family conflict is a type of its own. Its cause, its sharpening, its spread to non-participants, its form as well as the form of its reconciliation, are unique and not comparable to corresponding features in other conflicts, because the family quarrel proceeds on the basis of an organic unity which grows through a thousand inner and outer connections. Competition, however, is absent from its syndrome because family quarrels run directly from person to person: the indirect focus on an objective aim, characteristic of competition, may be added accidentally; it does not spring from the specific forces of the family.

---

3. Here, these two terms mean, approximately, "aim" and "provenience," respectively.—Tr.

COMPETITION IN RELIGIOUS GROUPS

THE SECOND SOCIOLOGICAL TYPE which excludes competition is exemplified in the religious community. Here the parallel efforts of all are directed toward a goal which is the same for all. But there is no competition because the attainment of the goal by one member does not exclude the others. At least according to the Christian conception, the house of God has room for all. And if grace does not reserve it for some while it gives it to others, it thereby proves the uselessness of competition.

This rather peculiar form and fate of parallel efforts might be called "passive competition." Pure manifestations of it are lottery and gambling. It is competition for a prize, but the essence of competition is absent: the difference of individual energies as the basis of winning or losing. The outcome here depends on some previous accomplishment, but differences in outcome do not depend on differences in this accomplishment.

Among the individuals grouped together by such a chance, this circumstance results in a highly specific relationship which, compared with competition proper, constitutes a novel mixture of equality and inequality of conditions. Where a number of people make exactly the same effort and have the same chance of success, while they know that a power they cannot influence, wholly gives or wholly withholds this success, they are characterized in a very specific fashion. On the one hand, they show an indifference quite unlike the relation among competitors, where success depends on the comparison of efforts. On the other hand, since the knowledge of winning or losing the prize on the basis of the quality of one's effort has a calming and objectifying effect upon one's feelings, here, where such knowledge is absent, envy and embitterment have their proper place. The loser does not hate but envy the person who is chosen by God or who wins at *Trente-et-Quarante*. Because of the mutual independence of their efforts, both "competitors" are here more distant and *a priori* indifferent toward each other than are competitors in an economic or sports fight. In the latter, it is the *deserved* failure which easily produces a characteristic hatred. It consists in the projection of our feeling of inadequacy unto the individual who has provoked it in us. The relation (always very loose) among the members of a group whose commonness is based on the grace dispensed by some divine, fateful, or human authority, is a specific mixture of indifference and latent envy—the envy coming to the surface once the decision is made, along with the corresponding feelings on the victor's part.

Yet no matter how great the difference between this configuration and the feelings of interaction that are characteristic of competition proper, nevertheless, every genuine competition probably contains a weaker or stronger admixture of this relationship which is determined by shared chances. It contains an appeal to a something in the power above the parties which decides by itself and is not guided by their efforts. The highly variable measure of this fatalistic admixture results in a specific gradation of competitive situations up to the type of chosenness by divine grace, where the admixture predominates and the factor of activity and differentiation, characteristic of competition as such, is absent.

Another apparent competition within the religious group is the jealous passion to surpass others in the attainment of the highest values. This passion often intensifies the accomplishments of obedience to rules, of meritorious works, of devotion, asceticism, prayers, donations. Yet it lacks the characteristic of competition, which is that the gain, *because* one obtains it, must be denied to the other.

Here is a sociologically notable difference between what may be designated as competition (*Wettbewerb*) and rivalry (*Wetteifer*). In every competition, even for the ideal values of honor and love, the significance of the success is determined by its proportion to the success of the competitor. Without changing at all, the winner's success would yet have a very different significance to him if the competitor's were greater rather than smaller than his. This dependence of absolute on relative success (or, to put it differently, of objective on personal success) motivates the whole competitive movement, but is wholly absent from the religious rivalry referred to. For here, the individual's activity is its own fulfillment; it would be unworthy of the highest justice or the supreme being to make the reward of the individual deed in any way depend on the fact that the merit of another individual is relatively greater or slighter. Instead, each is judged by *his* works, measured by transcendental norms. In competition, by contrast, he is judged by the works of the competitor, by the proportion of his own to the competitor's. In so far as the goal of a group has the *religious* possibility of being reached—an unconditional possibility, independent of the members' relations to each other—the group will not develop competition. This is equally true of all associations which are based on receptivity only and have no room for individually differentiated activities—such as scientific or literary clubs which limit themselves to organizing lectures; travel groups; association for Epicurean purposes.

COMPETITION, INDIVIDUALISM, AND SOCIAL INTEREST

IN ALL CASES discussed thus far, the particular purposes of the groups make for sociological forms which exclude competition. It is also possible, however, that certain reasons aside from these purposes and interests force the group to renounce competition or certain competitive means. Renunciation of competition altogether occurs in the measure of the predominance of the socialistic principle of the uniform organization of all work, or of the more or less communistic principle of the equality of all monetary return for work. Formally speaking, competition rests on the principle of individualism. Yet as soon as it occurs within a group, its relation to the social principle of the subordination of every individual interest under the uniform group interest is not at once clear. To be sure, the single competitor pursues his own purpose; he uses his energies for asserting his own interests. The competitive struggle is carried on by means of objective accomplishments, usually yielding a result which is somehow valuable to a third party. The purely social interest makes this result into an ultimate goal, while for the competitors themselves it is only a by-product. This social interest thus cannot only admit but may even directly evoke competition.

Competition, therefore, is by no means inseparably associated (as is easily thought) with the principle of individualism. According to this principle, the individual, his happiness, his achievement, and his perfection constitute the absolute meaning and purpose of all historical life. In regard to the question of ultimate purpose, competition is rather as indifferent as is any other mere technique. Hence it finds its contrast not in the principle of the exclusive social interest but only in another *technique*, also produced by that social interest—that is, socialism in the stricter sense of the word.

Socialism links two orientations. One is the orientation of institutions or at least of thought toward what is common to all, includes all, and to which everything individual must be subservient. The other is the orientation toward *organizing* all individual efforts. That is, socialism seeks to direct these efforts by means of a consistent, rational plan which excludes every friction among the elements, every waste of energy through competition, every accident of merely personal initiative. The result for the whole, therefore, is not produced through the antagonistic competition of spontaneously employed energies. It is brought about through a central directive which from the start organizes all for their mutual inter-penetration and supplementation—as it is most completely achieved in government bureaucracy or in factory personnel. This socialistic form of production is nothing but a technique for attaining the concrete purposes of happiness and culture, justice and perfection. It must therefore yield to free competition wherever competition emerges as the more suitable means.

SOCIALISM AND COMPETITION

THIS IS INDEED not a matter of political party affiliation only. It is the question whether the satisfaction of a need or the creation of a value is to be left to the competition of individual forces or to their rational organization, to their working against or for one another. This question calls for an answer in a thousand partial or rudimentary forms: in nationalization, cartellization, price competition, children's games. It arises in the problem whether science and religion produce deeper life values if ordered in a harmonious system or, on the contrary, if each of them tries to surpass the accomplishment presented by the other and is thus forced by this competition to develop its utmost effort. The question becomes important in the direction of theatrical plays. Is it more appropriate for the over-all effect to let each actor unfold his full individuality, intensifying and animating the whole by this competition of individual efforts, or is it better at once to let the over-all artistic image confine individuality to a smooth adaptation to that image? The question is reflected within the individual himself, when at one time he feels the conflict between ethical and aesthetic impulses, intellectual and instinctive solutions as the basis of the decisions which most truly and vividly express his real being, but at another time listens to these contradictory individual forces only in so far as he can incorporate them into a consistent life system guided by only one orientation.

Socialism in its ordinary sense of an economic-political tendency will not be fully understood if it is not recognized as the full-fledged and purified life-technique which, along with its opposite, is found, in beginnings and less clearly recognizable realizations, throughout the whole problem area of the management of complex affairs. The insight into the purely technical character of such orders ought to cause the socialistic organization to relinquish its claim to being a self-justifying aim and an ultimate value, and to calculate and appraise itself in comparison with individualistic competition in so far as it, too, is a means to super-individual ends. Yet it cannot be denied that our intellectual powers often fail in such an appraisal, and that decisions thus depend on the basic impulses of our individual natures. Considered from a purely abstract standpoint, these impulses, to be sure, produce only ultimate goals, while the means are determined by objective, theoretical insight. In practice, however, insight is not only so imperfect that the impulses must choose in its stead; it is also so weak that it cannot resist their persuasive power. Thus, the immediate attractiveness of the group form which is consistently organized and internally balanced and which excludes all frictions—such as this form has now become sublimated in socialism—will very often prevail beyond all rational justification over the rhapsodic, complexly split, and accidental character of the competitive form of production with its squandering of energy. In so far as individuals approach such a mood, they will exclude competition even in areas whose content is not opposed to it.

COMPETITION IN THE GUILD

THE SITUATION IS SIMILAR where the question is not the organic unity of the whole but the mechanical equality of the parts. The purest instance of this type is the constitution of guilds in so far as it rests on the principle that every master is to have "the same food." It is essential to competition that the equality among its elements continually shifts upward or downward. Each of two competing producers prefers the uncertain chance of differentiation to that certain half of the gain of which he can be sure if his and the other's offers are exactly alike. By offering other things or offering them in a different manner, he may, to be sure, profit from many fewer than half the consumers, but also perhaps from many more. The principle of chance which operates in competition so contradicts the principle of equality that the guilds held competition down by many prohibitions: against keeping more than one place of sale or more than a very limited number of apprentices; against selling anything but one's own product; and against offering quantities, qualities, and prices other than those fixed by the guild. How little the conditions of merchandizing itself required such restrictions became soon enough apparent when they could no longer be maintained: it was only the principle—both abstract and personal—of the equality of the gain which excluded the competitive form of production.

Further examples are not needed. The alternative which dominates innumerable areas and cases of human behavior, namely, whether a value should be fought over or be shared by agreement, is here manifest in the specific conflict-form of competition. Since here the parties do not wrestle with each other directly but fight for the success of their efforts before an outside authority, the sharing of the value consists in the voluntary equality of these efforts. Even the decision in favor of this equality does not only depend on the calculation of probability. For sometimes this calculus shows the greater gain to lie in the competitive chance with its oscillation between all and nothing, and sometimes in the safe but more restricted equality of effort. It is often enough the mood of a social epoch or the temperament of the individual which decides in favor of one or the other, aside from all rational calculation. Because of this affective (that is, general) character of the decision, the exclusion of competition often extends to areas where this is not required by objective considerations.

THE RESTRICTION OF
COMPETITIVE MEANS

OTHER MODIFICATIONS of social interaction occur when not competition as such, but only certain means of it are renounced, while competition itself continues. This is true in stages of development where the absolute competition of the animal struggle for existence changes into relative competition. It is the stage at which all frictions and paralyzations of forces which are not needed for purposes of competition proper are gradually eliminated. Neither the result nor the intensity of competition, however, is thereby affected. On the contrary, intensity is focused on the very result; it is no longer deflected into channels in which it would diminish the strength of both parties and thus both the subjective and objective utility of competition. This results in two forms, which may be called the inter-individual and the super-individual restriction of competitive means.

Inter-individual restriction of competitive means occurs when a number of competitors voluntarily agree to renounce certain practices of outdoing one another—whereby the renunciation by one of them is valid only so long as the other too observes it. Examples are the arrangement among booksellers of a given community to extend none or no more than five or ten per cent discount; or the agreement among store owners to close their businesses at eight or nine o'clock; etc. It is evident that here mere egoistic utility is decisive: the one does without those means of gaining customers because he knows that the other would at once imitate him if he did not, and that the greater gain they would have to share would not add up to the greater expenses they would likewise have to share. What is renounced here is thus not competition itself

—which always requires some sort of inequality—but those very points where no competition is possible because it would at once result in the competitors' equality.

Although hitherto this form has not often been observed in purity, it is of the greatest significance because it shows that it is possible for competitors to agree in the very area of competition without thereby weakening it in any way. By uncovering a point where their interests coincide, the antagonism of these interests is led all the more forcefully toward those points where it can freely develop. Such inter-individual restriction can grow indefinitely in order to free competition of all matters which are not really competition because they cancel each other out without effect. Since the means of competition consist for the most part in advantages offered to a third party, the third party has to this extent to bear the cost of the agreement to renounce those means.

In economics, the third party is the consumer; and thus it is clear how the road toward cartellization is taken. Once it is understood that one can do without many competitive practices provided the competitor does likewise, the result may be not only an ever intenser and purer competition, which has already been emphasized, but also the opposite. The agreement may be pushed to the point of abolishing competition itself and of organizing enterprises which no longer fight for the market but supply it according to a common plan.

This renunciaton of competiton has a very different sociological meaning from that in the guild discussed before. The guild left the individuals their autonomy; their equality required the descent of even the ablest among them to the level on which the weakest could compete with him; and such will inevitably be the form in which autonomous elements can attain mechanical equality. By contrast, cartellization takes as its start not the condition of the consumers but the objective efficiency of the enterprise. It is the extreme development of that restriction of competitive means which eliminates those that do not serve competitive purposes and eventually sheers the remainder of their competitive character. For, the complete domination of the market and the consumer's dependence gained therewith make competition as such superfluous.

LAW AND COMPETITION

RESTRICTING COMPETITIVE MEANS without affecting the continuation of competition itself finally may be brought about by authorities outside competition and its sphere of interest themselves, namely, by law and morality. In general, law denies competition only the means which are condemned in other relations among men as well: violence, damage to property, fraud, calumny. For the rest, competition is the kind of antagonism the forms and consequences of which are affected relatively less by legal restrictions than are those of other conflicts. If anybody were to destroy the economic, social, family, even physical existence of another by direct attack, as he may well do by means of competition—building a factory next to his, applying for a position along with him, submitting his entry in an essay contest along with his—the criminal code would at once interfere.

It is clear why matters exposed to ruin through competition are not protected. In the first place, because the competitors have no *intention* to destroy. None of them wants to achieve anything by his efforts but to carry off the prize. The fact that the other may perish in the process is only a by-product, entirely indifferent and perhaps regrettable to the winner. The second reason is that competition lacks the element of violation as such, and defeat and victory are only the appropriate and just expressions of the competitors' relative measures of strength. The victor exposes himself to exactly the same chances as does the vanquished; and the vanquished must therefore attribute his ruin to his own inadequacy alone.

Yet, as regards the first point, evil intent toward the damaged person is equally absent in a large number of criminal acts, actually in all of them which are not the product of revenge, malice, or cruelty. The bankrupt businessman who absconds with some property only wants to save something for himself, and the harm to his creditors' claims may well be a regrettable *conditio sine qua non* for him. The man who walks around in the streets shouting at night is punished for disturbing public peace even though he only wanted to vent his exuberant mood and never thought of robbing people of their sleep. To this extent, therefore, the person who ruins another through competition could at least be held responsible for having unintentionally caused the ruin. And exculpation in view of the equality of conditions, the voluntary nature of the whole action, and the justice with which the outcome of the competition follows the efforts expended, could equally well be adduced in respect to almost all kinds of conflict other than competition itself. If in a fist fight voluntarily entered into by two individuals under like conditions, one is badly hurt, the punishment of the other is to that extent no more logically consistent than would be the punishment of the businessman who has ruined his competitor by legitimate means.

The fact that this punishment does not occur has in part technical-legal reasons but above all the social-utilitarian reason that society does not want to give up the advantage which accrues to it from competition and which greatly outweighs the loss it suffers from the occasional destruction of individuals by the competitive struggle. This is the self-evident qualification of the French civil code on which the whole legal treatment of *concurrence déloyale* [disloyal competition] is based: "Any action by an individual which causes damage to another obliges the one by whose fault the damage has occurred to repair it." Society does not allow an individual to harm another directly and only to the harmer's benefit. It permits such harm, however, when it occurs while producing an objective result which is valuable to an indeterminable number of individuals. Similarly, the state would not permit officer duels if all they meant were the destruction of an individual on the basis of the personal interest of another, and if the inner cohesion of the officer corps did not draw from the idea of honor involved in the duel a strength which compensates the state for the sacrifice of the individual.

It is true that for some time French and German law has proceeded to restrict the means of competition in the interest of the competitors themselves. The fundamental intention is to protect the businessman from a competitor's advantages which could accrue to the competitor from the use of morally inadmissible means. Thus, all advertising designed to arouse the erroneous belief in the potential buyer that he is being offered more advantageous conditions than by anybody else is prohibited, even when the advertising does not actually force the public to pay a higher price for the merchandise. Further, it is prohibited to package merchandise so as to arouse in the buyer the illusion of a quantity not elsewhere obtainable at the price, even when the quantity actually sold is standard and adequate at that price. A third example is that a well-established firm with a large number of customers can now prevent somebody by the same name from bringing a product similar to its own on the market, if such action would make the customers believe that the new product is that of the old firm—no matter whether it is worse or better than the one with the original name.

What is interesting in these regulations is the apparently novel viewpoint of protecting the competitor who rejects unclean means of gaining customers, from the other competitor who wants to use such means. While elsewhere re-

strictions of business practices are designed to prevent the
public from being cheated, this is no motive of these regulations; yet the absence of this motive does not impede their
application. On more careful inspection, these prohibitions
are seen merely to make explicit the long existing law concerning fraud; and this explication is not only of legal but
also of formal-sociological interest. The German criminal
code punishes it as fraud if somebody, in order to gain material
advantages, "damages the property of another by arousing a misconception through misrepresenting facts." This is
naïvely understood to mean that the misconception must be
aroused in the same person whose property is to be damaged;
but the text of the law contains nothing regarding such an
identity. In permitting to prosecute as fraudulent the harming of A's property by arousing a misconception in B, the
law clearly covers that illegitimate competition. Through
it, a misconception is aroused in the public (without the
public suffering property damage), and the honest competitor
is harmed in his property; but no facts are misrepresented to
him. The businessman who fraudulently tells his buyer that
he is selling out because of a death in the family may not
harm him as long as he charges approximately the same sound
prices as his competitor does; but he harms that competitor
by perhaps robbing him of customers who in the absence of
that mendacious appeal might have remained faithful to him.
Thus the law is by no means a restriction of competitive
means as such, nor a specific protection of the competitors
from one another. The attitude of society toward competition is not characterized by the fact that it has recently applied
this restriction of competitive means but, on the contrary, by
the fact that it neglected to do so for so long—although this
restriction is merely the application of the extant criminal
law, in which it logically inheres.

There is something more. In respect to the motives behind
these laws it is always stressed that there is no desire to impose

any restrictions on honest competition but only to prevent competition which cheats the credulous customer. For our present purposes, this can be expressed more sharply by saying that these laws wish to eliminate from competition what is not competition in the social sense. For, competition in the social sense is a conflict which is fought out by means of objective accomplishments benefiting third parties. But the objective social criteria for deciding the outcome of competition are crossed and shifted through the application of such measures as advertising, appeal, and advantage through unclean devices. These means produce no objective asset but represent a kind of fight which is carried out *directly*, in a purely egoistic fashion, and not through socially useful channels.

What the law designates as "honest" competition turns out, on careful analysis, always to be what corresponds to that pure conception of competition itself. A commentary in the German code specifically excludes from "honest" competition the case where somebody builds a magnificent business next to a dress shop and undersells it long enough at prices made known through loud advertisements to ruin that small businessman. Looked at individualistically, this is the most brutal violence, and the relation between the two competitors certainly does not differ from that between a strong robber and a weak victim. Yet from the social standpoint, it is legitimate competition, that is, competition channeled exclusively through accomplishment and with a view at a third party—for even advertising, if it contains true statements, serves the public. What it contains in the way of misleading information, however, does not serve, even though it perhaps does not harm, the public; and it is at this point, therefore, that the protection of the competitor from violation can begin—*must* begin in order to keep the competing forces wholly within the pure, that is, social-utilitarian form of competition. Thus even the specific legal restrictions concerning competitive means reveal themselves to be, precisely, the restriction of those restrictions which competition suffers from purely subjective, individualistic practices.

MORALITY AND COMPETITION

IT SHOULD all the more readily be expected that here, as often elsewhere, law is supplemented by morality. Morality is not tied to social utility but very frequently regulates the behavior of men according to norms which lie below or above societal interests. It may regulate behavior according to the impulses of an immediate feeling interested exclusively in achieving peace with oneself and often finding such peace in the very opposition to the demands of society. Or it may regulate behavior according to metaphysical and religious ideas which sometimes include such demands but sometimes reject them completely as mere limited historical accidents. From both sources flow imperatives of interhuman behavior which are not social in the ordinary sense of the word—although they are sociological—and only by virtue of which the totality of human nature is found all over again in the ideal form of the Ought.

That ascetic, altruistic, fatalistic ethics reduce competition and its means as much as possible requires no discussion. The typical European moraltiy, however, has a more tolerant attitude toward competition than toward many other kinds of antagonism. This has to do with a particular combination of the characteristics which make up competition. As moral beings, we hesitate the less to employ our strength against an adversary, the greater our conscious distance between our subjective personality and the decisive effort we put into the fight. Where direct personal forces wrestle with one another, we are more easily subject to consideration and restraint and find it more difficult to resist appeals to charity.

In fact, within direct antagonisms, we are sometimes prevented by a kind of shame from unfolding our energies unreservedly, from playing all our cards, from investing our whole personality in a fight in which one personality stands against another. In struggles which are carried out in terms of objective accomplishments, these ethical-aesthetic delays do not interfere. For this reason, we can compete with individuals with whom we would at all costs avoid any personal controversy. By turning toward objects, competition attains the cruelty of all objectivity, a cruelty which does not consist in the enjoyment of the other's suffering but, on the contrary, in the elimination of all such subjective factors from the whole action. This indifference to the subjective element, characteristic of logic, law, and money economy, makes people who are not at all cruel practice all the harshness of competition—and with the certain consciousness of not wishing to do anything bad. The subjection of personality to the objectivity of procedure thus relieves moral conscience.

The same effect, however, can be achieved by the very opposite element in competition, namely, by the exact proportionality between the result of competition and the subjective energies of the individuals which they invest in it. Aside from deviations which have nothing to do with the nature of competition but derive from its interdependence with other forces and relationships, the result of competition is the incorruptible indicator of personal ability, which has become objectified in that result. We do not exploit what we gain through the favor of men or conjunctures, of accident or destiny we feel was pre-determined and occurs at the cost of others—we do not exploit such gains with as good a conscience as we exploit the result of our purely own actions. For beside the ethic of renunciation there is the ethic of self-assertion, and both have their common enemy in the fact that our relation to others is subject to external means, quite independent of the ego. Where finally, as in pure competition, this ego is decisive, our moral instinct is compensated for the mercilessness of competition by a satisfied feeling of justice—and not only the moral instinct of the victor but, under certain circumstances, even that of the vanquished.[4]

---

4. This is probably one of the points where the relation of competition to the characteristic features of modern life becomes apparent. Before the beginning of the modern period, man and his life task, or individuality and the objective content of its activities, appear in greater fusion and solidarity with one another, in more untrammeled mutual dedication, so to speak, than they do later. The last centuries have created a development of a previously unheard-of power and autonomy for objective interests, for objective culture. On the other hand, they have deepened to an equally unheard-of extent the subjectivity of the ego, the belonging-to-itself of the individual soul in the face of all objective and social claims. Modern man's sharply differentiated consciousness of object and of self lets the conflict-form of competition appear as if created for his specific requirements. It has the pure objectivity of procedure which owes its effects exclusively to its aim and to legal consequences, with complete indifference to the personality behind the process. And yet it also has the full self-responsibility of the person, the outcome's independence of individual strength—and precisely because personal effort is weighed, by impersonal powers, against personal effort. The most profound tendencies of modern life—the objective and the personal—find in competition one of their points of coincidence where they directly belong together in practice, thus showing their opposite characters to be mutually complementary elements of *one* unit in intellectual history.

Chapter Three

Conflict and the
Structure of the Group

THE DISCUSSION up to this point has shown numerous regularities among parties to a conflict—mixtures of antithesis and synthesis, superordination of one over the other, mutual restrictions as well as intensifications. But conflict has another sociological significance: not for the reciprocal relation of the parties to it, but for the inner structure of each party itself.

Daily experience shows how easily a quarrel between two individuals changes each of them not only in his relation to the other but also in himself. There are first of all the distorting and purifying, weakening or strengthening *consequences* of the conflict for the individual. In addition, there are the conditions of it, the inner changes and adaptations which it breeds because of their usefulness in carrying it out. Our language offers an extraordinarily telling formula of the essence of these changes: the fighter must "pull himself together" (*"sich zusammennehmen"*). That is, all his energies must be, as it were, concentrated in one point so that they can be employed at any moment in any required direction. In peace, the individual may "let himself go"—"himself" referring to the various forces and interests of his nature: they may be allowed to develop in various directions and independently of one another. In times of attack and defense, however, this would entail a loss of strength because of the counter-strivings of parts of his nature; and a loss of time because of the continual need for bringing them together and organizing them. The whole individual must therefore take on, as his inner position of conflict and chance of victory, the form of concentration.

CONFLICT AND THE CENTRALIZATION OF THE GROUP

THE FORMALLY SAME BEHAVIOR in the same situation is required of the group. This need for centralization, for the tight pulling together of all elements, which alone guarantees their use, without loss of energy and time, for whatever the requirements of the moment may be, is obvious in the case of conflict. It is so obvious that there are innumerable historical examples where such centralization supersedes even the most perfect peacetime democracy. Take, for instance, the well-known differences between the peacetime organization and the wartime organization of the North American Indians. Or take the London tailors who in the first quarter of the nineteenth century had a very different organization, one for peace and one for war with their employers. In quiet times, it consisted in small, autonomous, general assemblies in some thirty inns. In times of war, each inn had a representative; these representatives formed a committee which in turn elected a very small committee from which all commands issued and which was obeyed unconditionally. At that time, workers' organizations generally followed the principle of the interests of all to be decided by all. Here, however, necessity led to the formation of an organ of the strictest efficiency. It had a wholly autocratic effect, and its benefit was recognized by the workers without contradiction.

The well-known reciprocal relation between a despotic orientation and the warlike tendencies of a group rests on this formal basis: war needs a centralistic intensification of the group form, and this is guaranteed best by despotism. And vice versa: once despotism exists and that centralized form has materialized, the energies thus accumulated and pushed close together very easily strive after a natural relief, war with the outside. An example of the reverse of this connection may be mentioned because of its striking character. The Greenland Eskimos are one of the most anarchistic peoples, with no chieftainship whatever. When they fish, they like to follow the most experienced among them; but he has no authority, and there are no means of coercing an individual who isolates himself from the common undertaking of the group. It is reported of these people that the only way of fighting out quarrels among them is the singing contest. The person who believes himself harmed by another thinks up mocking verses against him and recites them at a tribal gathering especially called for the purpose; whereupon the adversary answers in similar fashion. The absolute lack of any warlike impulse is thus paralleled by the equally absolute lack of political centralization.

For this reason, the organization of the army is the most centralized among all organizations of the total group—with the exception, perhaps, of the fire department, which operates on the basis of formally parallel requirements. The army is the organization in which the unconditional rule of the central authority excludes any independent movement of the elements. Hence every impulse issuing from that authority is translated into the movement of the whole without any dynamic loss. On the other hand, that which characterizes a federation of states is its unit as a war-conducting power. In all other respects, the individual states may preserve their autonomies; in this one not, if there is to be a federation at all. The perfect federation of states may well be described as one which in its relations to other states (at bottom openly or latently warlike) forms an absolute unit, while in their relations to one another its members possess absolute independence.

THE BEHAVIOR OF
THE CENTRALIZED GROUP IN CONFLICT

IN VIEW OF the incomparable utility of unified organization for purposes of fight, one would suppose every party to be extremely interested in the opposed party's lack of such unity.[1] Nevertheless, there are some contrary cases. The centralized form into which the party is pushed by the situation of conflict grows beyond the party itself and causes it to prefer that the opponent, too, take on this form. In the struggles of the last decades between workers and employers, this has been most unmistakably the case. The Royal Labour Commission in England passed the decision in 1894 that the firm organization of the workers was favorable for the entrepreneurs in a given industry, and likewise that of the entrepreneurs for the workers. For, although the result of such organization was that an incipient strike could rapidly spread and last a long time, this was still more advantageous and economical for both parties than were the many local quarrels, work stoppages, and petty conflicts which could not be arrested in the absence of a strict organization of the employers and workers. This parallels war between modern states which, no matter how destructive and expensive, nevertheless results in a better over-all balance than do the incessant small conflicts and frictions characteristic of periods during which governments are less strongly centralized. In Germany too, workers had realized that a tight and effective organization of the employers, especially for the fighting out of interest conflicts, is of benefit to the workers themselves. For only an organization of this type can supply representatives with whom one can negotiate with full certainty. Only if there is such an organization can the workers in a given industry be sure that the success achieved is not at once put in jeopardy by disagreeing employers.

---

1. Cf. the earlier discussion of *Divide et impera* [see *The Sociology of Georg Simmel, loc. cit.*, Part Two, Chapter IV, Section 4, pp. 162-169].

The disadvantage a party suffers from the unified organization of its opponent—because this is an advantage for the opponent—is more than compensated for by the fact that if both parties are thus organized, their conflict itself can be concentrated, stay within their purview, and lead to a truly general peace for both. By contrast, if one finds oneself up against a diffuse multitude of enemies, one gains more often particular victories, but has great difficulty in achieving decisive actions which definitely fix the mutual relationship of the forces. This case is so deeply instructive in regard to the interdependence between the unitary form of the group and its behavior in conflict because it lets the efficacy of this interdependence triumph even over the immediate advantage of the enemy. It shows the objectively ideal form of organization for conflict to be that centripetality which the actual result of the fight brings out in the surest and fastest way. This teleology which, as it were, transcends the parties, allows each of them to find its advantage and achieves the seeming paradox that each of them makes the opponent's advantage its own.

THE EFFECT OF INTER-GROUP CONFLICT
ON THE GROUP

FOR THE SOCIOLOGICAL meaning of the formation of groups and group constellations, it makes an essential difference whether one or the other of the following two alternatives is the case. On the one hand, the group as a whole may enter into an antagonistic relation with a power outside of it, and it is because of this that the tightening of the relations among its members and the intensification of its unity, in consciousness and in action, occur. On the other hand, each element in a plurality may have its own opponent, but because this opponent is the same for all elements, they all unite—and in this case, they may, prior to that, not have had anything to do with each other; or they may have had, but now new groups emerge among them.

In respect to the first alternative, it must be emphasized that while the conflict or war of a group may let it overcome certain discrepancies and individual alienations within it, it often brings out these intra-group relationships with a clarity and decisiveness not otherwise reached. This can be observed particularly well in smaller groups which have not yet attained the degree of objectification characteristic of the modern state. If a political party which unifies many different directions of interest is pushed into a decisive and one-sided position of conflict, an occasion for secession results. In such situations, there are only two alternatives—either to forget internal counter-currents or to bring them to unadulterated expression by expelling certain members. If a family contains personalities among whom there are strong though latent discrepancies, then the moment when danger or attack pushes the family toward its tightest closing of ranks is that very moment which either secures its unity for a long time or destroys it permanently. It is the moment which decides with keen precision whether cooperation among such personalities is possible. If a school class plans a prank on the teacher or a fist fight with another class, all kinds of inner enmities are silenced; but on the other hand, certain students find themselves forced to separate from the rest not only because of objective motives but also because in such decisive attacks they do not wish to join certain others with whom they nevertheless do not hesitate to cooperate in other respects within the framework of the class. In short: the group in a state of peace can permit antagonistic members within it to live with one another in an undecided situation because each of them can go his own way and can avoid collisions. A state of conflict, however, pulls the members so tightly together and subjects them to such a uniform impulse that they either must completely get along with, or completely repel, one another. This is the reason why war with the out-side is sometimes the last chance for a state ridden with inner antagonisms to overcome these antagonisms, or else to break up definitely.

ELASTICITY AND RIGIDITY OF GROUPS IN THE FACE OF CONFLICT

HENCE GROUPS in any sort of war situation are not tolerant. They cannot afford individual deviations from the unity of the coordinating principle beyond a definitely limited degree. The technique for this is sometimes an apparent tolerance which is exercised in order to be able to expel with all the greater decisiveness those elements which definitely cannot be incorporated into the group. The Catholic Church has from the beginning actually found itself in a double state of war: against the whole complex of various doctrines which together make up heresy; and against the vital interests and powers in competition with the Church and claiming a sphere of power somehow independent of it. It attained the closed unitary front it needed in such a situation by treating dis-senters as long as possible as belonging to it, but the moment this was not possible any longer, expelling them with in-comparable energy. For group structures of this sort, a certain elasticity of their form is of the greatest importance,[2] not in order to achieve any changing over to the antagonistic forces or any reconciliation with them, but on the contrary, in order to contrast itself with them with the utmost sharpness while not losing any elements which it can in any way use. Elasticity here is no reaching beyond its own boundary. The boundary here confines the elastic body no less unambigu-ously than it bounds a rigid one. This expandability char-

2. On the elasticity of social forms in general, cf. the end of the chapter on self-maintenance [of the group; cf. "The Persistence of Social Groups," tr. Albion W. Small, *The American Journal of Sociology*, III: 662-698, March, 1898; 829-836, May, 1898; IV: 35-50, July, 1898; especially this last part].

acterizes, for instance, the monastic orders by means of which mystical or fanatical impulses of the Catholic Church (as of all religions) could live themselves out in a way completely harmless and unconditionally subordinate to it. In Protestantism, on the contrary, with its sometimes much greater dogmatic intolerance, these same impulses often led to separatist splinter groups which detracted from its unity.

MEN, WOMEN, AND CUSTOM

CERTAIN SOCIOLOGICAL ATTITUDES characteristic of women appear to go back to the same motive. Among the extremely complex elements that make up the over-all relation between men and women, there is a typical hostility which derives from two sources. As the physically weaker sex, women are always in danger of economic and personal exploitation and legal powerlessness[3]; and as the objects of the sensuous desire of men, they must always hold themselves on the defensive against the other sex. This fight, which pervades the inner and personal history of mankind, has rarely led to the direct cooperation of women against men. But there is a superpersonal form which serves as a protection against both of those dangers and in which the female sex is therefore interested, so to speak, *in corpore*: custom (*Sitte*). Its sociological nature has been characterized above [in the last section of Chapter II, on morality]; it must once more be shown in its application to the point under discussion.

A strong personality knows how to protect itself individually against attacks, or at most needs legal protection. The weak one would be lost even with legal protection if other, more powerful individuals did not somehow forego the exploitation of their superiority. They do this in part because

3. I am speaking here of the relationship as it has obtained throughout the overwhelmingly longest period of known history. I do not discuss the question whether the modern development of the rights and powers of women may invalidate this relationship in the future or has in part already done so.

of morality (*Sittlichkeit*). Since morality, however, has no other sanction than the individual's conscience, its effect is uncertain enough and needs complementing through custom. Custom, to be sure, does not have the precision and certainty of the legal norm, and yet it is guaranteed by an instinctive shyness and shame and by certain perceptibly disagreeable consequences of its violation. Custom is the essential protection of the weak who without it could not cope with the conflict of unrestricted forces. Its character, therefore, is on the whole prohibitive, restrictive. It effects a certain equality between the weak and the strong which in restraining the purely natural relationship between the two may even go so far as to prefer the weak—as is shown, for instance, in chivalry. The fact that in the creeping conflict between men and women, men are stronger and more aggressive, forces women under the protection of custom and makes them its custodians—they are called to this office, and called to it by their own interest. This of course also commits them to the most rigorous observance of the whole complex of the prescriptions of custom even where they do not directly concern male transgressions: all customary norms are related to one another through solidary interpendence, since the violation of a single one weakens the principle and thus every other. For this reason, women usually hold together in this respect without reservation. An actual unity corresponds to that peculiarly ideal unity in which men lump them together when they simply speak of "the women." The contrast between the sexes fully has the character of a *party* contrast. This sex-linked solidarity which women have in the eyes of men was expressed long ago by Freidank:

Man bears his shame alone,	(*"Der Mann trägt seine Schmach allein,*
But let a woman fall,	*Doch kommt ein Weib zu Falle*
The blame rests on them all.	*So schilt man auf sie alle."*)

The solidarity has a real vehicle in its interest in custom as its common means of fight. It is for this reason that we finally come to see here a repetition of the sociological form under discussion. In respect to a particular woman, women as a rule know only complete inclusion or else complete exclusion from the realm of custom. They have the tendency as much as possible not to admit, or to interpret as harmless, a breach of custom by a woman (except where love of scandal and other individual motives counteract this). But if this is no longer possible, they render an irrevocable and unconditionally harsh judgment of exclusion from "good society." If the breach of custom must be admitted, the culprit is radically eliminated from that unit which is held together by its common interest in custom. It occurs, therefore, that women pass the same judgment of condemnation on Gretchen, Marguerite Gautier, Stella, and Messalina without permitting differences, and thus the possibility of mediation, between those within and those outside custom. Women's position on the defensive does not allow the wall of custom to be lowered even at a single point. Their party, in principle, knows no compromise but only absolute acceptance of the individual woman into the ideal totality of "decent women" or her equally absolute exclusion from it. The purely moral justification of this alternative is by no means beyond all doubt; it can only be understood in terms of the unbreachable unity which a party unified by a common opponent must impose on its members.

INTERNAL AND EXTERNAL OPPOSITION AND GROUP COHESION

FOR THE SAME REASON, a political party may benefit from a decline in its membership, as long as this decline purifies it of elements which tend to mediation and compromise. Two conditions must usually be met if this is to be the case: a situation of acute conflict, and a relative smallness of the fighting group. The model is the minority party, especially if it does not limit itself to the defensive. English parliamentary history shows this in several instances. When, for instance, in 1793 the Whig party was already melted down greatly, it was strengthened by the defection of all elements which were still somehow mediating and lukewarm. The few remaining, very resolute personalities were only then enabled to engage in a wholly united and radical political action. The majority group does not have to insist on such decisiveness of pro and con. Vacillating and conditional members are less dangerous to it because its large volume can afford such peripheral phenomena without being affected in its center. But where, as in the smaller group, the periphery is closer to the center, every uncertainty of a member at once threatens the core and hence the cohesion of the whole. The slight span between the elements makes for the absence of that elasticity of the group which here is the condition of tolerance.

For this reason, groups, and especially minorities, which live in conflict and persecution, often reject approaches or tolerance from the other side. The closed nature of their opposition without which they cannot fight on would be blurred. This has been shown more than once in, for instance, the denominational struggles in England. Both under James II and under William and Mary, the Non-Conformists and Independents (Baptists, Quakers) were occasionally approached by the government, but they did not welcome these approaches by any means. For they offered to the more yielding and undecided members among them the temptation and possibility of forming intermediate positions or at least of attenuating their contrast. Every concession of the other side, which is only partial anyway, threatens the uniformity in the opposition of all members and hence the unity of their coherence on which a fighting minority must insist without compromise.

Hence the unity of a group is often lost when it has no longer any opponent, as has been stressed in various discussions of Protestantism. It has been said that since to "protest" is necessary for it, Protestantism loses its energy or inner unity once the adversary against whom it protests gets out of range. It lost inner unity even to the point of repeating within itself the conflict with the enemy, by breaking up into a liberal and an orthodox party. In similar fashion, in the history of political parties in the United States, the complete submission of one of the two great parties has several times had the effect of dissolving the other into sub-groups and party oppositions. Nor is it at all advantageous for the unity of Protestantism not to have any real heretics.

By contrast, the consciousness of unity of the Catholic Church has been decisively strengthened by the fact of heresy and the aggressive behavior against it. The irreconcila-bility of their opposition to heresy has permitted the various elements within the Church, as it were, to orient themselves and to remember their unity, despite certain divergent inter-ests. A group's complete victory over its enemies is thus not always fortunate in the sociological sense. Victory lowers the energy which guarantees the unity of the group; and the dissolving forces, which are always at work, gain hold. The decay of the Western Roman Empire in the fifth century has been explained by the subjugation of its common enemies. Perhaps its basis—protection on the one hand, dedication on the other—had no longer been quite natural for some time, but became apparent only when no common enmity ele-vated the whole above its inner contradictions. Within cer-tain groups, it may even be a piece of political wisdom to see to it that there be some enemies in order for the unity of the members to remain effective and for the group to remain conscious of this unity as its vital interest.

CONFLICT AS THE BASIS
OF GROUP FORMATION

THE LAST EXAMPLE leads to cases of an intensified cohesive function of conflict. Conflict may not only heighten the concentration of an existing unit, radically eliminating all elements which might blur the distinctness of its boundaries against the enemy; it may also bring persons and groups together which have otherwise nothing to do with each other. The powerful effect of conflict in this respect emerges probably most clearly in the fact that the connection between conflict situation and unification is strong enough to become significant even in the reverse process. Psychological associations generally show their strength in their retroactive effect. If, for instance, we imagine a given person under the category of "hero," the connection between the representation of the person and of the hero is most intimate if we cannot think of the category of hero without the automatic, simultaneous emergence of the image of that personality.

In similar fashion, unification for the purpose of fighting is a process which is experienced so often that sometimes the mere collation of elements, even when it occurs for no purpose of aggression or other conflict, appears in the eyes of others as a threatening and hostile act. The despotism of the modern state was directed above all against the medieval idea of unification. Eventually, every association as such— whether between cities, estates, knights, or any other elements of the state—appeared to the government as a rebellion, as a latent fight against it. Charlemagne prohibited guilds as sworn associations and explicitly permitted them for charitable purposes, without oath. The emphasis of the prohibition lies on the sworn obligation even for legitimate purposes, because these legitimate purposes can easily combine with others which are dangerous to the state. Thus, the Moravian land order of 1628 says: "Accordingly, to enter or erect federations or unions, for whatever purpose and against whomever they may be conceived, is not permitted to anybody but the king." The fact that the ruling power itself sometimes favors or even launches such associations does not contradict this connection, but confirms it. This is so not only if the association is to counteract an existing opposition party (where it is obvious), but also in the more interesting case when it is designed harmlessly to distract the general tendency to associate. After the Romans dissolved all political associations of the Greeks, Hadrian created an organization of all Hellenes (*koinón synédrion ton Hellénon*) for ideal purposes: games and commemorations—for the maintenance of an ideal, wholly unpolitical pan-Hellenism.

For the direction taken by the relationship under discussion, historical cases are so close at hand that the only point worth insisting upon is the observation of the *degrees* of unification which are possible through conflict. Uppermost is the establishment of the unified state. Essentially, France owes the consciousness of its national unity only to its fight against the English, and only the Moorish war made the Spanish regions into one people. The next lower grade of unification is constituted by confederacies and federations of states, with additional numerous gradations according to their cohesion and the measure of power of their central authorities. The United States needed the War of Independence; Switzerland, the fight against Austria; the Netherlands, rebellion against Spain; the Achaean League, the struggle against Macedonia; and the founding of the new German Empire furnishes a parallel to all of these instances.

Here also belongs the formation of unified estates. The element of conflict (latent and open contrasts) is of such evident significance for them that I only mention a negative example. The fact that Russia has no proper aristocracy as a closed estate would seem to be bound to favor the broad and unrestrained development of a bourgeoisie. In reality, the opposite is the case. If, as elsewhere, there had been a powerful aristocracy, it certainly would have put itself in frequent opposition to the prince, who in turn would have depended upon an urban bourgeoisie. Evidently, among the princes such a conflict situation would have aroused an interest in developing a unified bourgeois class. The bourgeois themselves found no militant stimulus (in this case, no stimulus at all) to close ranks as an estate. If they had, they could have gained from the conflict by joining one or the other side.

In all positive cases of this type, it is characteristic that the unity, while it originates in conflict and for purposes of conflict, maintains itself beyond the period of struggle. It comes to have additional interests and associative forces which no longer have any relation to the initial militant purpose. In fact, the significance of conflict consists in the articulation of the latent relationship and unity; conflict is more the occasion of unifications which are required internally than it is the purpose of these unifications. To be sure, within the collective interest in conflict, there is a further gradation, namely, according to whether the unification for the purpose of conflict refers to attack *and* defense or to defense only. Unification for the exclusive purpose of defense probably occurs in most coalitions of extant groups, especially when the groups are numerous and heterogeneous. This defense purpose is the collectivistic minimum, because even for the single group and the single individual it constitutes the least avoidable test of the drive for self-preservation. Evidently, the more numerous and varied are the elements which associate, the smaller is the number of interests in which they coincide—in the extreme case, the number is reduced to the most primitive urge, the defense of one's existence. Thus, in reply to the entrepreneurs' fear that all English trade unions might unite one day, one of their most ardent adherers pointed out that even if it came to that, it could only be for purposes of defense.

In comparison with these cases in which the collectivizing effect of conflict transcends the moment and the immediate purpose of the group (and this may happen even in regard to the minimum just mentioned), the extent of this effect is slighter when the unification occurs only *ad hoc*. Two types must be distinguished here. On the one hand, there is association for a single action. Frequently, especially in wars properly speaking, this claims the total energies of its elements. It creates a unit without residue; but after achieving or failing to achieve its immediate objective, this unit lets its parts go back to their former separate existence—as, for instance, did the Greeks after eliminating the danger from the Persians. In the second type, the unity is less complete but also less transitory. Here, the elements are grouped around a war aim which is singular, not so much in terms of time as in terms of content, and which does not cause any contact among them other than in this one respect. Thus there has been in England a Federation of Associated Employers of Labour, founded in 1873 to fight the influence of trade unions; and a few years later, a similar association was formed in the United States in order to counteract strikes, no matter in what branch of industry.

The character of both types of unification appears of course most pointed when it is composed of elements who at other times or in respects other than the one at issue are not only indifferent but hostile toward one another. The unifying power of the principle of conflict nowhere emerges more strongly than when it manages to carve a temporal or contentual area out of competitive or hostile relationships. Under certain circumstances, the contrast between ordinary antagonism and momentary association for purposes of fight can be so pointed that it is precisely the depth of the mutual hostility of the parties which forms the direct cause of their joining up. In the English parliament, the Opposition has sometimes been formed when the extreme partisans of the ministerial policy were not satisfied with the administration and joined their radical opponents with whom they were connected by the common antagonism against the ministry. For instance, under Pulteney, the Ultra-Whigs united with the High-Tories against Robert Walpole. It was precisely

the radicalism of the principle of enmity against the Tories
which united its adherents with the Tories: had their anti-
Toryism not been so fundamental, they would not have
joined their enemies in order to bring about the fall of the
Whig minister who for them was not Whiggish enough.

This case is so extreme because the common adversary
brings otherwise mutual enemies together; in the view of
each of these enemies, he, their common adversary, leans too
much toward the other side. But this extreme case is only
the purest example of the trivial experience that even the
bitterest enmities do not prevent an association if this association is directed against a *common* enemy. This is particularly true if both or at least one of the parties now cooperat-
ing has very concrete and immediate goals, and all that is
needed to attain them is the removal of particular adversaries.
French history from the Huguenots to Richelieu shows that
it was sufficient for one of the internal parties to increase its
hostility to Spain or England, Savoy or the Netherlands, and
the other at once joined this foreign power—without regard
to the harmony or disharmony between that power and its
own positive aims. These parties in France, however, had
very concrete goals and only needed "room," freedom from
the opponent. They were thus ready to join up with any
opponent of that opponent if only he had the same intention,
in utter disregard of their usual relations with him. The
more purely negative or destructive a given enmity is, the
more easily will it bring about a unification of those who
ordinarily have no motive for any community.

The lowest step in this scale of unifications on the basis of
conflict, their least acute form, is constituted by associations
which are held together only by a common mood. In such
cases, members know that they belong together in so far as
they have a similar aversion or similar practical interest against
a third party. This interest, however, does not necessarily
lead to a common aggression against that party. Here too,

two types must be distinguished. The first is illustrated by the opposition between masses of workers and few employers in large-scale industry. In the struggle for working conditions, this situation evidently produces not only particular, really effective coalitions among the laborers, but also the quite general feeling that they all belong together somehow because they all are united in the basically identical struggle against the employers. To be sure, at certain points this feeling is crystallized in particular actions of political party formation or wage struggles. Yet as a whole, it can by its own nature not become practical. It remains the mood of an abstract belonging-together by virtue of common opposition to an abstract adversary. Here, then, the feeling of unity is abstract but lasting.

In the second type, it is concrete but temporary. This second type is exemplified when persons who are not acquainted with each other but who share the same level of education or sensitivity, find themselves together, perhaps in a railroad car or under similar circumstances, with others of crude and vulgar behavior. Without any scene, without so much as exchanging a word or glance with each other, they still feel like a party, held together by their common aversion to the vulgarity (which is aggressive at least in the ideal sense) of those others. This unification, with its extremely tender and delicate, though wholly unambiguous character, marks the extreme on the scale of unifications of completely alien elements through a common antagonism.

The synthetic strength of a common opposition may be determined, not by the number of shared points of interest, but by the duration and intensity of the unification. In this case, it is especially favorable to the unification if instead of an actual fight with the enemy, there is a permanent *threat* by him. In regard to the first period of the Achaean League, that is, around 270 B.C., it is emphasized that Achaea was surrounded by enemies, all of whom, however, had something else to do than attack it. It is said that such a period of danger which always threatened but never materialized, was especially apt to strengthen the feeling of unity.

This is a case of a peculiar type: a certain distance between the elements to be united, on the one hand, and the point and interest uniting them, on the other, is a particularly favorable constellation for unification, notably in large groups. Religious relations are a case in point. In contrast to tribal and national deities, the world-spanning God of Christianity has an infinite distance from the believers. He is entirely without features related to the specific character of the individual. In compensation, however, he can comprise even the most heterogeneous peoples and personalities in an incomparable religious community. Another illustration: dress always characterizes certain social strata as belonging together; and it seems to fulfill this social function best when it is imported from abroad. To dress as one dresses in Paris, means to have a close and exclusive association with a certain social stratum in other countries—already the prophet Zephaniah speaks of noblemen as wearing foreign clothes.

The very manifold meanings connoted by the symbol "distance" have much psychological affinity with one another. For instance, an image the object of which is in any sense represented as "distant" seems almost always to have a more impersonal effect. If accompanied by such a representation, the individual reaction following from immediate closeness and touch is less poignant, has a less immediately subjective character, and thus can be the same for a larger number of individuals. The general concept which covers a number of particulars is the more abstract (that is, the more distant from each of the particulars), the more numerous and different from each other these particulars are. Just so, a point of social unification at a greater distance from the elements to be unified (both in a spatial and in a figurative sense) likewise appears to have specifically unifying and comprehensive effects. Unification by a more chronic than acute danger, by an always latent but never exploding conflict, will be most effective where the problem is the lasting unification of somehow divergent elements. This was true of the Achaean League I already mentioned. In the same vein, Montesquieu remarks that while peace and confidence are the glory and security of monarchies, republics needs somebody they fear. This observation is apparently based on a feeling for the constellation discussed. Monarchy itself sees to it that possibly antagonistic elements are held together. But when such elements have nobody above them to enforce their unity but instead enjoy relative sovereignty, they will easily break apart unless a danger shared by all forces them together. Evidently, such a danger can last and can guarantee a permanent group structure only by a permanent threat of conflict, rather than through a single, open fight.

While this is more a question of degree, the basic connection between collectivity and hostility requires the following additional comments. From their very origin, aggressive, much more than peaceful, enterprises tend to solicit the cooperation of the largest possible number of elements which would otherwise remain scattered and would not have started action on their own account. On the whole, people engaging in peaceful actions usually limit themselves to those who are close to them in other respects as well. For "allies," however—and linguistic usage has indeed given a warlike color to this intrinsically neutral concept—one often enough accepts elements with whom one hardly has, or even wants to have, anything in common. There are several reasons for this. First, war, and not only political war, often constitutes an emergency in which one cannot be choosy about friends. Secondly, the object of the action lies outside the territory or periphery of the allies' other immediate interests, so that after the fight is over they can return to their earlier distance.

Thirdly, while gain by means of fight is dangerous, if the fight is successful, the gain usually is quick and intensive. Hence for certain elements, it has a *formal* attraction which peaceful enterprises can engender only through a particular *content*. Fourthly, in conflict, the specifically personal element in the fighter recedes; and thus the unification of otherwise wholly heterogeneous elements is possible. Finally must be noted the motive of the easy reciprocal stimulation of hostility. Even *within* a group which feuds with another, all kinds of latent or half-forgotten hostilities of its members against those of the other group come to the fore. In this way, war between two groups usually evokes in a third group much ill will and resentment against one of the two. By themselves, these feelings would not have led to an outbreak, but now that another group has led the way, as it were, they cause the third group to join it in its action. It is quite in line with this that in general, convergent relations among *peoples as wholes*, especially in earlier times, existed only for purposes of war, while other relations, such as trade and commerce, hospitality, and intermarriage, only concerned *individuals*. Agreements between the peoples made these individual relationships possible, but did not themselves initiate them.

MAN'S NEED FOR ACCENTUATION

WHEN A HISTORICAL DEVELOPMENT occurs in the form of a continuous rhythmical change between two recurring periods, each of them as important as the other and attaining its own meaning only through its relation and contrast with it, then the consistent image we form of such a process rarely reflects the objective regularity and the persistent level on which its elements alternate. Instead, we almost inevitably bestow on the change of these elements a teleological accent so that one of them is always the point of origin, which is objectively primary, while the other develops out of it; and the renewed transition of the second to the first appears to us as a kind of regression.

For instance, we represent the world-process as an eternal change between the qualitative homogeneity of fused masses of matter and their differentiated dispersion. We may well be convinced that always the one comes out of the other and then again the reverse takes place. Yet because of the way in which our conceptual categories happen to function, we think of the undifferentiated state as of the first. That is, our need for explanation requires us to derive variety from unity much more than vice versa. Even so, objectively it would perhaps be more correct to posit neither as first but to assume an infinite rhythm where we cannot stop at any stage we have calculated but where we must always derive that stage from an earlier, opposite one. It is similar in regard to the principles of rest and motion. The two follow each other endlessly—whether we look at the whole of being or at particular sequences of it. Nevertheless, we usually feel the state of rest to be the original, or definitive, state, which itself needs no derivation, as it were. Thus whenever we look at a pair of periods together, one of them always seems to be the explanatory and the other the derived one; it is only in such a rank ordering that we believe to grasp the meaning of their dynamic process. We are not satisfied with their mere alternation, as it actually shows itself, without designating one of its elements as primary and the other as secondary. Man is too much of a discriminating, valuing, purposive being not to articulate the uninterrupted flow of alternating periods by means of such accents; not to interpret them in analogy to domination and submission, or preparation and fulfillment, or transitory and definitive states.

THE TRANSITION FROM CONFLICT TO PEACE AND FROM PEACE TO CONFLICT

THIS ALSO APPLIES to conflict and peace. Both in the succession and in the simultaneity of social life, the two are so interwoven that in every state of peace the conditions of future conflict, and in every conflict the conditions of future peace, are formed. If one follows historical developments back in time from this standpoint, one cannot stop anywhere. In historical reality, each of the two conditions uninterruptedly relates itself to the other. Nevertheless, we "feel" an inner difference into this sequence of the links of the chain: conflict appears as preliminary, with peace and its contents as the purpose of it. While from an objective viewpoint, the rhythm of the two elements pulsates evenly on the same level, our valuation articulates, as it were, iambic periods, with war as thesis, and peace as arsis. Thus, in the oldest constitution of Rome, the king must ask the citizens for their consent when he wants to start a war, but he needs no such consent—which is thus presupposed as a matter of course—when he wants to make peace.

This example by itself is enough to suggest that the transition from war to peace constitutes a more serious problem than does the reverse. For the transition from peace to war really needs no particular examination: in peace, the situations out of which open conflict develops themselves are conflict in a diffuse, imperceptible, or latent form. For instance, the economic superiority (because of their slave economy) of the Southern American states before the Civil War over the Northern states was itself the reason for that war. Yet as long as such a situation causes no antagonism but is a matter of the internal conditions of the two territories, it remains outside the specific question of war and peace. The moment, however, the situation took on the color of war, it itself turned out to be an accumulation of antagonisms, of attitudes of hatred, newspaper polemics, frictions between private persons, frictions at the borders, and reciprocal moral suspicions in areas outside the central point of conflict. The end of peace thus is not signaled by a specific sociological situation. Antagonism, though not at once in its most explicit or strongest form, rather develops directly out of whatever the objective conditions of peace may be.

It is different with the opposite sequence. Peace does not follow conflict with the same directness. The ending of conflict is a specific enterprise. It belongs neither to war nor to peace, just as a bridge is different from either bank it connects. The sociology of conflict thus requires, at least as an appendix, an analysis of the forms in which a fight terminates. These forms constitute interactions not to be observed under any other circumstances.

MOTIVES FOR ENDING CONFLICT

THERE IS PROBABLY nobody who does not know the formal attraction of war and of peace. Because each of them exists in a certain measure, out of them grows the additional attraction of change between them. Individuals differ from one another only by the rhythm of the alternation they require, by the parts of it they feel as ups and downs, by their own initiative with which they provoke it or their mere expectation of it as a gift or curse of fate. For this reason, the motive for ending a conflict—longing for peace—is something much richer than mere tiredness of fighting. It is the rhythm which at a given moment causes us to ask for peace as a very concrete state—something much more than the absence of conflict.

This rhythm, however, must not be understood in a wholly mechanistic sense. It has been said, to be sure, that intimate relations, such as love and friendship, need occasional quarrels in order to be reminded of the happiness by the contrast with the discord they suffered; or in order to interrupt the closeness of the relationship—which, after all, has some-

thing coercive and enclosing for the individual—by an aliena-
tion which removes this pressure. It is probably not the
deepest relationships which need such a turn. Probably it
is required more by cruder natures, who must be stimulated
by coarse differences and whose short-breathed lives favor
violent contrasts. They are the type of "enemies today,
friends tomorrow" ("*Pack schlägt sich, Pack verträgt sich*");
they need discord in order to preserve the relationship. The
very intimate and refined relation continues without such
antagonistic intervals. It finds its attraction-by-contrast in
the surrounding world, in the disharmonies and hostilities of
life outside itself. They are sufficient as background for its
internal peace.

Among the indirect motives of the desire for peace—
clearly to be distinguished from those discussed thus far—
are two. On the one hand, there is the exhaustion of strength,
which can simply place the need for peace beside the continuing desire to fight. On the other hand, there is the deflection of interest from conflict to a higher object. The
second type produces various kinds of moral feints and
self-deceptions: the parties do as if they buried the battle
axe because of an ideal interest in peace, or they actually
believe this; whereas in reality the issue of the fight has
merely lost its interest, and they only want to free their
energies for other purposes.

THE TERMINATION OF CONFLICT
THROUGH THE DISAPPEARANCE
OF ITS OBJECT

IN DEEP-FOUNDED RELATIONS, the end of conflict occurs
by their undeflectible basic current returning to the surface,
thus smoothing the counter-currents. The situation is quite
different when the conflict is ended by the disappearance of
its object. Every conflict which is not absolutely impersonal
uses the available energies of the individuals who participate

in it. It acts like a point of crystallization around which these forces arrange themselves at greater or smaller distances, analogously to the arrangement of core and auxiliary troops. It thus gives the whole complex of the fighting personality a peculiar structure. If conflict is ended in one of the ordinary manners—victory and defeat, reconciliation, or compromise —this psychological structure forms itself back into that of the state of peace. The transition of the central point from excitation to rest communicates itself to the other energies which participated in the fight. This process by which the movement of conflict ebbs out internally, has an organic course, even though it is infinitely varied.

Instead, however, the process may also be wholly irrational and turbulent. This happens in case the object of the conflict is suddenly eliminated so that the whole movement, so to speak, swings into the void. The main reason for this is that our feeling is more conservative than is our mind. Emotional excitement does not come to rest by any means the moment our mind recognizes that its occasion no longer exists. Whenever psychological currents which have their origin in a certain content, are suddenly robbed of this content, there is confusion and harm. They no longer can develop and live themselves out naturally. Deprived of all basis, they feed on themselves or try to seize upon a meaningless surrogate object. Examples of accidents or higher powers which deprive an ongoing conflict of its aim are: a rivalry where the person or party decides in favor of a third party; a fight over a booty which in the meantime is taken by somebody else; or a theoretical controversy where the problem is unexpectedly solved by a higher intelligence and both conflicting positions are shown to have been wrong. If such circumstances rob a conflict of its object, an empty continuation of the quarrel, a sterile mutual accusing, a revival of earlier, long-buried differences often takes place nevertheless. This is the swinging-on of the movement of conflict, which must fight itself out in some fashion—here a wholly senseless and tumultuous fashion—before it can come to rest. It is perhaps most striking in cases where both parties recognize the object of the conflict as illusory and not worth fighting for. Here shame over our error often makes us continue the fight for a long time, with a wholly groundless and strenuous expenditure of energies, but with all the greater bitterness against our opponent who forces us into this quixotism.

VICTORY

THE SIMPLEST and most radical way of getting from fight to peace is victory. Victory is a unique phenomenon. Although it has innumerable individual forms and degrees, it does not resemble anything else that can occur among human beings and is called by other names. Among the many varieties of victory which give the peace that follows it a particular color, I only mention one. It is that kind which is brought about not exclusively by the superiority of one of the parties but, at least in part, by the resignation of the other. This giving-in, this declaring oneself conquered, this accepting the victory of the other over oneself before all strength and possibility of opposition are exhausted, is not always a simple phenomenon. It can be brought about by a certain ascetic tendency, by the pleasure of self-humiliation and of giving-oneself-up. Such a tendency is not strong enough to make one yield at once without fight; but it becomes manifest as soon as the mood of the victor begins to "catch"—it may even find its most subtle fascination in the contrast with the fighting spirit which was alive only a moment earlier.

The decision to yield may also be brought about by the feeling that it is nobler to give up than to cling, to the very end, to the improbable chance that things may take a turn for the better. To throw away this chance and at this

price to escape the fate of having one's own defeat demonstrated in all its inevitability and in all detail, has something
of a great and noble style. It is characteristic of persons
who are certain not only of their strength but also of their
weakness, without having to assure themselves of them all
the time in a tangible manner. Finally, in this voluntary
character of declaring oneself vanquished lies an ultimate
proof of one's power. This last deed, at least, one can still
do: one actually makes a gift to the victor. In personal conflicts it can therefore be observed sometimes that the yielding of a party before the other has conclusively made its
case, is felt by the more powerful one as a sort of offense:
it is as if it actually were the weaker of the two and the
other had for some reason yielded without having had to.[4]

COMPROMISE

IN SHARP CONTRAST to the termination of conflict through
victory is its end in compromise. In a classification of conflicts, one of the most important characteristics is their intrinsic accessibility or inaccessibility to such ending. This is
by no means decided only by the question of whether the
prize of the conflict is an indivisible unity or can be divided
among the parties. In respect to certain objects, compromise

---

4. This belongs in the area of forms of relations in which accommodation
(*Entgegenkommen*) is an offense (*Zunahetreten*). There are enough cases
where politeness is offensive: gifts which humiliate; concern out of pity,
which has the effect of impertinent intrusion or increases the pain of its
victim; good deeds where the enforced gratitude or the relationship caused
by them is more painful than is the need the good deeds satisfy. The fact
that such sociological constellations are possible goes back to the frequent
and deep discrepancy which exists between the objectively expressible and
specifically conceptualized content of a situation or of some behavior, on
the one hand, and, on the other, its individual realization which it attains
as a mere element of a richly complex life totality. This is the formula for
the differences between treating the sickness or the sick person, between
punishing crime or the criminal, between the teacher's transmitting a
content of culture or educating the pupil. Objectively, in terms of their
conceptual content, many things are beneficial, while as individually experienced realities they are the opposite.

through division is out of the question. This is true among rivals for the favor of a woman; among parties interested in the same indivisible object which is for sale; also in struggles which have hatred and revenge as their motive. Yet even fights over indivisible objects may be accessible to compromise—in case, that is, these objects can be *represented*. If so the prize, properly speaking, can only go to one of the conflicting parties; but the winner rewards the other for his yielding by a substitute value.

The question of whether goods are functional in this fashion does not, of course, depend on some objective equivalence among them, but on the inclination of the parties to end the antagonism by means of concessions and indemnifications. The chance that this occurs lies between two extremes. One is the case of pure stubbornness. Here the most rational and generous indemnification, for which the party would ordinarily like to give up the prize of the struggle, is rejected merely because it is offered by the opponent. The other extreme is the case where a party first seems attracted by the specific character of the prize at issue. But then, nevertheless, it gives it up to the other with perfect equanimity, being compensated for it by an object whose capacity to replace the original remains a riddle to any outsider.

On the whole, compromise, especially that brought about through exchange, no matter how much we think it is an everyday technique we take for granted, is one of mankind's greatest inventions. The impulse of both uncivilized men and children is to grasp every object that pleases them, whether or not it is already in somebody else's possession. Robbery, along with gift, is the most obvious form of change in ownership. Under primitive conditions, robbery and gift rarely occur without fight. The fight can be avoided by offering the owner of the desired object another object from one's own possession. This makes the over-all effort much smaller than it would be if the fight were continued or begun. To realize this fact is the beginning of all civilized economy, of all higher commerce. All exchange of things is a compromise. To be sure, the poverty of things, in comparison with purely psychological and spiritual matters, is attested to by the fact that the exchange of things always presupposes yielding and resignation. In contrast, love and all contents of the mind can be exchanged without any enrichment having to be paid for by impoverishment. Under certain social conditions, it is considered chivalrous to rob and to fight for booty, while exchange and purchase are looked down upon as undignified and vulgar. This is due in part to the compromise character of exchange, to the fact that it involves concession and renunciation, which makes it the very opposite of fight and victory.

Every exchange presupposes that valuations and interests have taken on an objective character. The decisive element is no longer the mere subjective passion of desire, to which only fight is adequate, but the value of the object which is recognized by both sides and which, objectively unchanged, can be expressed by several other objects. Renunciation of the valued object, because one receives the value quantum contained in it in some other form, is the means, truly miraculous in its simplicity, of accommodating opposite interests without fight. This means presumably required a long historical development, because it presupposes a psychological separation of a general feeling for values from the specific object with which it was fused originally, a rise above imprisonment by immediate desire. Compromise through representability, of which exchange is a special case, means the fundamental, even though only partly realized, possibility of avoiding conflict or of terminating it before the mere strength of the parties has sealed the decision.

CONCILIATION

FROM THE OBJECTIVE CHARACTER of ending conflict through
compromise, conciliation is distinguished as a purely subjective method. Here I do not refer to conciliation as a
consequence of compromise or other accommodation of conflict, but to conciliation as the cause of ending conflict. Conciliability is a primary mood. Quite aside from objective
reasons, conciliability tries to end conflict just as much as
quarrelsomeness, no less without any objective occasion, supports it. This wholly elementary and irrational tendency to
conciliation is probably at work in the innumerable cases in
which conflict does not end as the most merciless consequence of power relations. It is something quite different
from weakness, gullibility, social morality, or love for one's
fellowman; it is not even identical with peacefulness. For,
peacefulness avoids fight from the start, or carries it on,
once it is forced upon it, accompanied by the constant
undercurrent of the need for peace. Conciliability, on the
contrary, often emerges in its full, specific nature precisely
after complete devotion to a fight.

Its psychological and sociological character seems most
closely akin to that of forgiving (*Verzeihen*). After all,
forgiving, too, does not presuppose any laxity of reaction
or lacking strength of antagonism. It too is lit up in all its
purity after the most deeply felt wrong and the most passionate struggle. Hence in both conciliation and forgiving
lies something irrational, something like a denial of what
one still was a moment before. This mysterious rhythm of
the soul which makes processes of this type depend precisely and exclusively on the processes which contradict
them is perhaps most clearly revealed in forgiving. For, forgiving is probably the only affective process which we
assume without any question to be subordinate to the will
—otherwise, the *begging* of foregiveness would be meaningless. A request can only move us to something over which

the will has power. That I spare the vanquished enemy or renounce all revenge on the individual who has offended me, can understandably be achieved on the basis of a request: it depends on my will. But that I *forgive* them, that is, that the feeling of antagonism, hatred, separateness yield to another *feeling*—in this respect, a mere resolution seems to be as powerless as it is in respect to feelings generally. Actually, however, the situation is different, and cases where we *cannot* forgive even with our best will are very rare.

If one wants to go to the bottom of the phenomenon of forgiving, one finds that it contains something which rationally is not fully comprehensible. To a certain extent, conciliation too partakes of this character. This is why both of these sociological processes find themselves transferred in a significant fashion into the mysticism of religion. They owe the possibility of this transfer to the fact that even as sociological phenomena they contain a mystically religious element.

The "reconciled" relation, as against the relation which has never been broken, presents a special problem. Discussion now does not refer to relationships which were treated earlier. They were relations whose inner rhythm itself vacillated between discord and conciliation. Instead we are now concerned with those which suffer a real break but afterward come together again as if on a new basis. Few features are as decisive in characterizing them as is the answer to the question whether their intensity is increased or diminished in such a case. This at least is the alternative for all more profound and sensitive natures. For whenever a relation after a radical rupture is revived as if nothing had happened, this generally reveals either a more frivolous or a cruder mentality.

The second case—decreased intensity—is the least complex. It is readily understandable that a discord, once it has occurred, can never be overcome entirely even with the most honest efforts of the parties concerned, and even if no part of the object of conflict is left behind and no irreconcilability whatever exists. The mere fact that there once was a break at all is decisive. In intimate relations which suffered from extreme discord, there is an additional element which brings such a result about. The parties have seen that they can get along without each other, that life went on, though perhaps not very gaily. This not only reduces the value of the relationship. It also is precisely this—after the unity has been reconstituted—for which the individual easily reproaches himself as for a kind of treason and disloyalty which can never be made good again. It weaves into the re-established relation the participants' lack of courage, and a distrust of their own feelings.

Yet this often involves self-deception. The surprising relative ease with which we can sometimes bear the break-up of an intimate relatonship derives from the excitement we still retain from the catastrophe, which vitalized in us all kinds of energies whose momentum carries us on and supports us a while longer. The death of a beloved person does not unfold its whole terror in the first hour. Only time brings us into all the situations in which that person used to be an element and through which we must now live as with a torn-out limb; no first moment can anticipate them in summary fashion. In the same way, an important relation is not dissolved during the first moment of its break-up when rather the *reasons* for its dissolution dominate our consciousness. Instead, we feel our loss every single hour only from case after case of it. For this reason, it often is only after a long time that our feeling does justice to it, while during the first moment, it seemed to bear its loss with a certain equanimity. For this reason too, the conciliation of certain relationships is more profound and passionate the longer the breach lasted. And for this reason it becomes understandable generally that the *tempo* of the conciliation, of "forgiving and forgetting," is of great significance for the further structural development of the relationship. It becomes clear that those terminations of conflict do not really eliminate the conflict if its latent forces have not found some outlet beforehand: the conciliatory tendency truly penetrates them only when they attained a more open or at least more conscious stage. Just as we must not learn too fast if what we learn is to remain with us, we also must not forget too fast if forgetting is to unfold its sociological significance to the fullest extent.

There are various causes for the reverse phenomenon, where the measure of intensity of the reconciled relationship grows *beyond* that of the unbroken one. The chief characteristic is the fact that the breach has created a background against which all values and all perpetuations of the union now stand out more consciously and clearly. Further, the discretion with which one evades all reference to the past conflict produces a new delicacy, even a new, unspoken communion in the relationship. For everywhere, the common avoidance of an all too sensitive point can mean as much intimacy and mutual understanding as can the lack of inhibition which makes every object of the individual's inner life a matter of positive sharing. Finally, the intensity of the desire to protect the revived relation against any shadow derives not only from the suffering of the breach which has been experienced, but above all from the consciousness that a second breach could not longer be healed as the first was. At least for sensitive persons, this would in innumerable cases make a caricature of the whole relation. Even the most deep-founded bond can come to a tragic breach and to conciliation. But this belongs to those occurrences which in the same form can take place only once; their repetition robs them of all dignity and seriousness. For once a first repetition has occurred, there is nothing to prevent a second and third, which would make all the excitements of the process banal and drag them down to the level of a frivolous game. For more refined natures, the feeling that a second breach would be definitive—a feeling for which there hardly exists any analogy before the first breach has occurred—is perhaps the strongest bond which distinguishes the reconciled relationship from one that has never been broken.

IRRECONCILABILITY

THE DEGREE of reconcilability following upon conflict or suffering, inflicted unilaterally or mutually, thus has a deep significance for the development of relations among people. It is because of this very significance that *ir*reconcilability, the negative extreme of reconcilability, also partakes of that significance. It too, like its positive counterpart, can be a formal psychological disposition. To be sure, it needs an external situation to be actualized; but then it emerges quite spontaneously and not only as the consequence of other, intermediary feelings. Both tendencies belong among the fundamental polar elements whose mixtures determine all relations among men. It is sometimes said that if one cannot forget, one cannot forgive and not fully reconcile oneself. If this were true, it would mean the most horrible irreconcilability. For it would make conciliation depend upon the disappearance from consciousness of every occasion of its opposite. And furthermore, like all processes which rest on forgetting, conciliaton would be exposed to the perpetual danger of being revoked. If the statement is to have any sense at all, it is the reverse: where the state of conciliation exists as a primary fact, it is the cause which prevents the discord and pain one has inflicted on the other from ever again rising to consciousness.

Correspondingly, true irreconcilability does not consist in the failure of consciousness to overcome past conflicts—this failure is rather the consequence of irreconcilability. Irreconcilability means that through the conflict, the soul has undergone a modification of its *being*. This modification is irrevocable. It must be compared with a lost limb, not with a scar. This is the most tragic irreconcilability: neither a grudge nor any reservation or secret spite needs to remain to put a positive barrier between two individuals—only because of the conflict fought through, something has been killed which cannot be revived, not even with the most passionate effort. Here is a point where the powerlessness of the will over man's actual being becomes glaringly manifest—in strongest psychological contrast to the type of forgiving touched upon before.

This is the form irreconcilability takes on in very homogeneous and not too easily movable persons. There is another form, characteristic of internally very differentiated individuals. Here, image and after-effect of the conflict and of everything for which one had to reproach the other continue in consciousness and cannot be forgotten. But around all of this grow that undiminished love and affection in which those memories and renunciations do not figure as losses. Instead, like organic elements, they are incorporated into the image of the other. We now love him while including, so to speak, these liabilities in the balance of our total relationship to him—just as we love a person with all his faults, which we perhaps "wish away" but cannot "think away" from him. The bitterness of the conflict, the points where the personality of the other has failed—the points which have brought a permanent resignation or an ever renewed irritation into the relationship—none of this is forgotten; all, really, remains unreconciled. But it is localized, as it were; it is taken, as one factor, into the total relationship, whose central intensity does not necessarily suffer therefrom.

It is evident that these two forms of irreconcilability, which are clearly different from those usually called by that name, nevertheless include their whole range. In one of them, the result of the conflict, completely detached from its particular contents, sinks into the very center of the personality and reorganizes it in its deepest layer in so far as the personality relates to the other. In the other form, by contrast, the psychological precipitate of the conflict is, as it were, isolated. It remains a specific element which can be taken into the image of the other, to be included in the over-all relation to him. Obviously, between that worst and this easiest form lies the whole variety of degrees to which irreconcilability places peace under the shadow of conflict.

The Web of
Group-Affiliations[1]

TRANSLATED BY REINHARD BENDIX

1. Translation of "Die Kreuzung sozialer Kreise," *Soziologie* (Muenchen: Duncker & Humblot, 1922), pp. 305-44. The title of this chapter, "Die Kreuzung sozialer Kreise," has not been translated. A literal translation of this phrase, "intersection of social circles," is almost meaningless. What Simmel had in mind was that each individual is unique in the sense that his pattern of group-affiliations is never exactly the same as that of any other individual. He may belong to a different set of groups as compared with another person, and even if he belonged to the same groups, he would still orient himself or he would define his situation (in the terms of W. I. Thomas), with reference to groups or social categories, which distinguish him from the other. (This has recently been elaborated by Robert K. Merton and others under the heading "reference group theory.") And because the same individual belongs to many groups, Simmel refers to him as "standing at the intersection of social circles."

Two further comments may prove helpful to the reader. In using the word "circle" as a synonym for "group," Simmel often plays with geometric analogies; it has seemed advisable to me to minimize this play with words in so far as this seemed compatible with an accurate rendering of Simmel's thought. I have used the term "group-formation" when Simmel refers to the origin of a "social circle," and the term "group-affiliation" when he has in mind that an individual "belongs to a social circle." I would ask the reader to keep in mind that in Simmel's view these terms should be interpreted broadly. He speaks, for example, of women as a social circle or group, not only when they "form" a group or are "affiliated" with one, but also when they perform a given social role in society.

Phrases in square brackets have been added, when this seemed necessary for clarity. All sub-headings have been added also. The footnotes are Simmel's when marked by the initials G.S., and the translator's when marked R.B. Unmarked footnotes are sentences from Simmel's text which have been made into footnotes for the sake of clarity.

ANALOGIES BETWEEN PERCEPTION
AND GROUP-FORMATION

THE DIFFERENCE between thinking in its advanced and its primitive form is shown in the different motives which determine the association of ideas. To the primitive mind any accidental coexistence of objects in time and space is psychologically sufficient to lead to a connection between ideas. At first, that unification of attributes, which makes up a concrete object, seems to be a unified whole. But [upon examination it appears that] each composite attribute is closely connected with other attributes which together make up that specific environmental context in which one has come to know them. To become conscious of a concrete object [as a configuration of these attributes and] as a distinct conception is possible only when the idea [of the object] occurs in many different connections. Then the likeliness and the interrelation among these connections becomes clearly evident, and the conception of the object frees itself more and more from its ties with attributes which are actually different and which were bound together with the object only through an accidental coexistence. Thus, the association of ideas is no longer a simple response to what is actually perceived. Instead, it becomes grounded in the content of what is perceived, and more complex concepts are developed upon this basis. In this manner there emerges the likeness or similarity of the attributes [which make up a concrete object] and these attributes are consequently disentangled from their various accidental and irrelevant connections.

The development which takes place among ideas finds an analogue in the relationship of individuals to each other. At first the individual sees himself in an environment which is relatively indifferent to his individuality, but which has implicated him in a web of circumstances. These circumstances impose on him a close coexistence with those whom the accident of birth has placed next to him. This close coexistence represents the first condition of the phylogenetic and ontogenetic development, whose continuation aims toward the association of homogeneous members from heterogeneous groups. Thus, the family comprises a number of different individuals, who are at first entirely dependent on this familial association. However, as the development of society progresses, each individual establishes for himself contacts with persons who stand outside this original group-affiliation, but who are "related" to him by virtue of an actual similarity of talents, inclinations, activities, and so on. The association of persons because of external coexistence is more and more superseded by association in accordance with internal relationships. Just as a higher concept binds together the elements which a great number of very different perceptual complexes have in common, so do practical considerations bind together like individuals, who are otherwise affiliated with quite alien and unrelated groups. New contacts are established between individuals which penetrate every nook and cranny of the contacts that are earlier, relatively more natural and that are held together by relationships of a more sensual kind.

PROPINQUITY AND INTEREST
AS A BASIS OF GROUP-FORMATION

THE INDEPENDENT GROUPS, whose alliances used to constitute universities at an earlier time, were divided according to the nationality of the students. Later on, so-called faculties were developed in the place of such alliances. These faculties were academic departments according to common areas of study. Thus, a group whose cohesion depended upon geographic and physiological factors, *terminus a quo*, was entirely replaced by a group whose cohesion was based on purpose, on factual considerations, or, if one will, on individual interests.

The development of the English trade unions shows the same pattern, though its characteristics were somewhat more complex. Originally, the individual trade unions tended towards local exclusiveness: they were closed to workers who came from elsewhere. Frictions and petty jealousies between such separate groups were unavoidable. However, the tendency toward a uniform organization of trades throughout the country gradually eliminated this situation. The following example shows that this change had become inevitable. When the cotton weavers decided upon uniform piece rates, it was apparent that this would lead to a concentration of the industry in favorably located places and to losses for the more remote villages. Yet, even the representatives of these remote villages voted for uniform piece rates because this was deemed best for the industry as a whole.

Although from the beginning workers came together on the basis of their similar activities, their association depended largely on the fact that they were neighbors. Unquestionably this contributed to a close contact between a specific trade and the associations of the other trades, as long as the latter existed in the same locality. In the course of its development the association of workers in one trade was removed from this dependence on local relationships. Henceforth, the similarity in the occupation of the members became the only determinant of the relationship between the association and those in other trades. An historian of the trade unions has expressed this change by saying that the *trade* had become the governing principle of the workers' organizations in place of the *city*. There is an element of freedom operating here: for however much confinement there may be in the position of the worker, membership in a trade union implies more freedom of choice for the individual than belonging to the citizenry of a town.

In general, this type of development tends to enlarge the sphere of freedom: not because the affiliation with, and the dependence on groups, has been abandoned, but because it has become a matter of choice with whom one affiliates and upon whom one is dependent. Any association, which is based on local relationships or is otherwise brought about without the individual's participation, differs from affiliations which are freely chosen, because as a rule the latter will make it possible for the individual to make his beliefs and desires felt. Hence, such groupings may be based upon relationships which grow out of the nature of the individuals concerned.

PRIMARY GROUPS
AND MILITARY ORGANIZATIONS

IN ORDER TO BUILD a stable organizational structure, it is often expedient to utilize relationships which have arisen in this manner, though the purpose of the organization may diverge markedly from the causes which prompted its initial development. Among the Syssitians of Sparta, fifteen men sat at one table according to free choice. *One* vote was sufficient to bar a man from joining the table. This "company of the table" [Tischgenossenschaft] was then made the basic unit of the army. Here the actual tendencies and sympathies of the individuals intermingled with the ties of neighborhood and of kinship as the basis for the formation of a primary, communal group. The army organization, for which these tendencies and sympathies of individuals were utilized, was extremely strict and impersonal. Yet, the option of the Syssitian fellowship formed a flexible link between the army and the equally impersonal ties of locality and of kinship. The rational meaning of the table-company, based on free choice, buttressed the rationality of the army organization, which was established along entirely different lines. However, the unconditional prerogative of the military organization broke down the clan-organization of the Spartans, quite apart from the special technique of establishing the units of the army. In the rest of Greece it was a given clan or local district which constituted a military unit. Only in Sparta did the objective interest of the military break down this bias [of locale or of kinship]; there the unit of military organization was determined according to purely military considerations.

Even among primitive peoples, for example in Africa, one can observe how the organization of government along lines of war-like centralization has destroyed the clan-organization of the tribe. Since women in general represent the principle of indigenous family-solidarity, we can explain thereby the enmity against everything feminine and the social impotence of women in military organizations. Nevertheless, a matriarchy among war-like peoples may develop with relative frequency. On the one hand, it may develop out of the explicit separation of civil and military affairs. On the other hand, it may result from psychological motives: the warrior is tyrannical and brutal at home, to be sure, but he is also tired and lazy. He is satisfied if his wants are taken care of and someone else has the governing power. But these conditions of civil society have nothing to do with those purposive [primarily military considerations], which destroy the clan and create a new, purely rational structure from its fragments.

The decisive fact is that the warriors form an organized whole entirely on a military basis and without regard to any other interests. In other respects these warriors may be separated from one another by quite different [personal] relations which would be irrational only if these other relations would affect the military organization. The choice of comrades among the Syssitians of Sparta meant that freedom was a principle of efficient organization, which is not often the case. For in this case the qualities of the individual personality became the determinants of group-solidarity. Compared with the usual reasons, this is a completely new, revolutionary and clearly intelligible basis of solidarity, even if it is arbitrary and irrational in specific instances.

It is in this sense that the principle of "free association" prevailed in the last three centuries of the middle ages in Germany. In the earliest times of free village communities the solidarity of men was a matter of local development. Then, the feudal era created quite a different external basis of unity stemming from the relationship of the men to *one* lord. Only the principle of "free association" made the will of the associated individuals the basis of unity. It is obvious that the community-life of individuals must have assumed very peculiar forms as those earlier bases of unity were replaced. These bases had appeared as preordained, they had molded the individual and were not initiated by him, but they were subsequently eliminated or thwarted by the spontaneous actions of the individual.

AFFILIATION WITH TWO GROUPS
OF DIFFERENT TYPE

THE UNITY of a group [which is based on "voluntary association"] is of a later type. It grows out of a more primitive type, but need not always be of a more rational character. The consequences for the external position as well as for the internal make-up of the individual will have a special character if both types [of establishing unity] are founded upon equally deep-seated causes that lie beyond the control of the individual.

The Australian aborigines, whose cultural position is very primitive, live in small, rather close-knit tribes. But the entire population is divided into five *gentes* or totemic associations in such a way that members of the various gentes are found in each tribe and each gens extends over several tribes. Within the tribe the members of the same totemic association do not engage in collective action. Rather, the fact of their membership becomes an element in all other groups, however defined, and as such these members of the totemic association constitute an extended family. If in a fight between two hordes the members of the same totem meet, they avoid each other and seek out another opponent, which is likewise reported of the Mortlack Islanders. Sexual relations take place between men and women according to the conditions of the gentes, even though they are members of different tribes and have never met in any other way. Those wretched people are quite incapable of engaging in rational, collective action, properly so-called. But by belonging to two such sharply divided groups [the gens and the tribe] they must experience an enrichment of their lives, a tension and a doubling of their vitality, which they could probably not attain otherwise.

In modern family life a somewhat similar affiliation [with two divided groups] is often established by virtue of the solidarity among members of the same sex, though the content and the effect [of this affiliation] are of a very different kind. For example, a mother's instincts will cause her to side with her son as her own kin on occasions when she is drawn into the disputes between himself and his wife. But on another occasion her instincts may cause her to take the side of her daughter-in-law as a member of her own sex.[2] To belong to the same sex is one of the causes for collective action, which pervades social life perennially, and which intermingles with all other causes of collective action in the most varied ways and degrees. The fact that two persons are of the same sex will, as a rule, act as an organic and natural [cause of collective action] in contrast to which other causes [of collective action] have something of the individual, intentional, and conscious about them. However, in the case referred to, one may sense perhaps that the relationship between mother and

---

2. Of course, this applies only in so far as her instincts are acted out *a priori,* and without regard to all the individual nuances of the case.

son is the natural and effective one, while the solidarity of one woman with another is of a secondary and deliberate nature, which is more significant in an abstract than in an existential sense. Yet, to be of the same sex is sometimes a cause of solidarity, which is peculiar in the sense that it is primary, fundamental, and independent of all arbitrary decisions. Yet, this solidarity can become effective only through mediation, reflection and conscious striving. Hence, these much later and accidental causes function in fact as the first and unavoidable cause of group-formation.

ORGANIC AND RATIONAL CRITERIA
OF GROUP-FORMATION

IN RELATIVELY UNCOMPLICATED situations age groups may function as a sociological criterion and may become a basis of division for the entire group. Like the division between the sexes, age groups stand midway between the organic and the rational. For example, in Sparta around 200 B.C. political parties were designated as the elders, the young men, and the youngsters. Similarly, among different primitive peoples one finds men organized in age-groups, each of which has a special social significance and a special way of life. The basis of this solidarity is entirely personal and impersonal at the same time.

Obviously, age-groups provide such a basis of solidarity only when the culture is still without an extensive intellectual life. For this would immediately foster the unfolding of individual intellectual differences, of differences in the development of ideas, of political parties depending on ideologies. And as a result individuals of quite different age-groups would feel that they belong together. It is, indeed, this lack of an acquired education which is one of the reasons why youth as such shows a certain solidarity, why young people are attracted to one another much more so than are older people.

Youths are often surprisingly indifferent towards each other's individuality.

The division by age-groups is a cause, though an extremely awkward cause, of group-formation, which combines personal and objective criteria. The organic and rational causes of group-formation, whose contrast is usually emphasized, are here brought together. A purely physiological aspect of individuals, their age, becomes a basis for joint action. Individuals are consciously brought together on this basis. Age is an entirely natural and personal fact which here works as a completely objective principle. It is understandable that this fact gains great importance for the social structure of primitive peoples, since age is relieved of all elements of caprice, since the fact of age is immediately apparent and as such readily determines one's outlook on life.

Group-affiliations which are formed according to objective criteria constitute a superstructure which develops over and above those group-affiliations which are formed according to natural, immediately given criteria. One of the simplest examples is the original cohesion of the family-group which is modified in such a way that the individual member introduces his family into other groups. One of the most complex examples is the "republic of scholars" which is in part an intellectual and in part a real association of all persons, who join in the pursuit of such a highly general goal as knowledge. In all other respects these scholars belong to the most varied groups—with regard to their nationality, their personal and special interests, their social position, and so on.

The period of the Renaissance demonstrated most clearly the power of intellectual and educational interests to bring together in a new community like-minded people from a large variety of different groups. Humanistic interests broke down the medieval isolation of social groups and of estates. They gave to people who represented the most diverse points of view and who often remained faithful to the most diverse occupations, a common interest in ideas and in knowledge. This common interest, whether one of active pursuit or of passive appreciation, cut across all previously established forms and institutions of medieval life. Humanism at that time entered the experience of all peoples and groups from the outside as something that was equally strange to all. And this very fact made it possible for Humanism to become a common area of interest for them all, or at any rate for certain people among them.

For example, the idea prevailed that all things famous belonged together. This is shown by the collections of biographies which began to appear in the 14th century. These biographies described in a single work people of excellence from many fields, whether they were theologians, or artists, statesmen or philologists. In their way, the secular rulers gave recognition to this new rank-order, which involved a new analysis and synthesis of social groups. Robert of Naples befriends Petrarch and makes him a gift of his own purple cape.

Two hundred years later this social action has shed its lyric guise and has assumed a more objective and strictly limited form. Francis I of France wanted to make that social group, which was concerned exclusively with the higher learning, completely independent and autonomous even in relation to the universities. These universities were charged with the education of theologians and jurists. But Francis I proposed a separate academy, whose members would devote themselves to investigation and teaching without having any practical purpose in mind. It was a consequence of this separation of what is intellectually significant from every other value that the Venetian Senate accompanied the extradition of Giordano Bruno with this letter to the Papal Court. Bruno was one of the worst heretics, it said, he had done the most reprehensible things, he had led a dissolute, even a devilish life. In other respects, however, he was one of the most distinguished intellects that could be imagined, a man of rare learning and spiritual greatness.

The restlessness and the adventurous spirit of the Humanists, their often unstable and unreliable character, were in keeping with the independence of the intellect, which was the central focus of their lives. This independence made them indifferent to all other obligations usually incumbent upon men. The individual humanist spent his life in a colorful variety of life-situations. This way of life was symbolic of the movement of Humanism, which embraced the poor scholar and the monk, the powerful General and the brilliant Duchess, in a single framework of intellectual interests. Thereby the way was opened for a most important, further differentiation of the social structure, though there are precedents for such a development in antiquity.

Criteria derived from knowledge came to serve as the basis of social differentiation and group-formation. Up to the Renaissance, social differentiation and group-formation had been based either on criteria of self-interest (economic, military, and political in a broad or narrow sense), or of emotion (religious), or of a mixture of both (familial). Now, intellectual and rational interests came to form groups, whose members were gathered from many other social groups. This is a striking example of the general trend, that the formation of groups, which has occurred more recently, often bears a rational character, and that the substantive purpose of these groups is the result of conscious reflection and intelligent planning. Thus, secondary groups, because of their rational formation, give the appearance of being determined by a purpose, since their affairs revolve around intellectually articulated interests.

MULTIPLE GROUP-AFFILIATIONS
WHICH ARE NOT IN CONFLICT

THE NUMBER of different social groups in which the individual participates, is one of the earmarks of culture. The modern person belongs first of all to his parental family, then to his family of procreation and thereby also to the family of his wife. Beyond this he belongs to his occupational group, which often involves him in several interest-groups. For example, in an occupation that embraces both supervisory and subordinate personnel, each person participates in the affairs of his particular business, department office, etc., each of which comprises higher and lower employees. Moreover, a person also participates in a group made up of similarly situated employees from several, different firms. Then, a person is likely to be aware of his citizenship, of the fact that he belongs to a particular social class. He is, moreover, a reserve-officer, he belongs to a few clubs and engages in a social life which puts him in touch with different social groups. This is a great variety of groups. Some of these groups are integrated. Others are, however, so arranged that one group appears as the original focus of an individual's affiliation, from which he then turns toward affiliation with other, quite different groups on the basis of his special qualities, which distinguish him from other members of his primary group. His bond with the primary group may well continue to exist, like one aspect of a complex image, which retains its original time-space coordinates though the image itself has long since become established psychologically as an objective configuration in its own right.

During the Middle Ages the individual had certain typical opportunities of group-affiliation, over and above his citizenship in his community. The Hansa League was an association of cities, which permitted the individual to participate in a wide range of activities that not only extended beyond each individual city but far beyond the boundaries of the German

Reich. Likewise, the medieval guilds were not organized in accordance with the jurisdiction of towns; instead, affiliation of the individual with the guild had no reference to his status as a citizen within a town but involved him in an organization extending throughout all of Germany. And journeymen-associations extended beyond the boundaries of the guilds, just as the guilds extended their jurisdiction beyond the boundaries of the towns.

These patterns [of group-affiliation] had the peculiarity of treating the individual as a member of a group rather than as an individual, and of incorporating him thereby in other groups as well. An association which is derived from the membership of other associations places the individual in a number of groups. But these groups do not overlap and the problems which they entail for the individual, differ from the problems posed by the sociological constellations which will be discussed subsequently. Group-formation during the Middle Ages was inspired by the idea that only equals could be associated, however often the practice deviated from the theory. This idea obviously was connected with the completeness with which medieval man surrendered himself to his group-affiliation. Hence, cities allied themselves first of all with cities, monasteries with monasteries, guilds with related guilds. This was an extension of the equalitarian principle, even though in fact members of one corporate body may not have been the equals of members from an allied group. But as *members of a corporate body* they were equals. The alliance was valid only in so far as this was the case, and the fact that the members were individually differentiated in other respects was irrelevant. This way of doing things was extended to alliances between *different* groups, but these groups were regarded even then as equal powers within the new alliance. The individual as such was not a fact in such an alliance; hence his indirect participation in it did not add an individuating element to his personality. Nevertheless, as will be discussed later, this was the transitional step from the medieval type to the modern type of group-formation. The medieval group in the strict sense was one which did not permit the individual to become a member in other groups, a rule which the old guilds and the early medieval corporations probably illustrate most clearly. The modern type of group-formation makes it possible for the isolated individual to become a member in whatever number of groups he chooses. Many consequences resulted from this.

GROUP-AFFILIATIONS AND
THE INDIVIDUAL PERSONALITY

THE GROUPS WITH WHICH the individual is affiliated constitute a system of coordinates, as it were, such that each new group with which he becomes affiliated circumscribes him more exactly and more unambiguously. To belong to any one of these groups leaves the individual considerable leeway. But the larger the number of groups to which an individual belongs, the more improbable is it that other persons will exhibit the same combination of group-affiliations, that these particular groups will "intersect" once again [in a second individual]. Concrete objects lose their individual characteristics as we subsume them under a general concept in accordance with one of their attributes. And concrete objects regain their individual characteristics as other concepts are emphasized under which their several attributes may be subsumed. To speak Platonically, each thing has a part in as many ideas as it has manifold attributes, and it achieves thereby its individual determination. There is an analogous relationship between the individual and the groups with which he is affiliated.

A concrete object with which we are confronted has been called the synthesis of perceptions. And each object has a more enduring configuration, so to speak, the more various the perceptions are, which have entered into it. Similarly as individuals, we form the personality out of particular elements of life, each of which has arisen from, or is interwoven with, society. This personality is subjectivity par excellence in the sense that it combines the elements of culture in an individual manner. There is here a reciprocal relation between the subjective and the objective. As the person becomes affiliated with a social group, he surrenders himself to it. A synthesis of such subjective affiliations creates a group in an objective sense. But the person also regains his individuality, because his pattern of participation is unique; hence the fact of multiple group-participation creates in turn a new subjective element. Causal determination of, and purposive actions by, the individual appear as two sides of the same coin. The genesis of the personality has been interpreted as the point of intersection for innumerable social influences, as the end-product of heritages derived from the most diverse groups and periods of adjustment. Hence, individuality was interpreted as that particular set of constituent elements which in their quality and combination make up the individual. But as the individual becomes affiliated with social groups in accordance with the diversity of his drives and interests, he thereby expresses and returns what he has "received," though he does so consciously and on a higher level.

As the individual leaves his established position within *one* primary group, he comes to stand at a point at which many groups "intersect." The individual as a moral personality comes to be circumscribed in an entirely new way, but he also faces new problems. The security and lack of ambiguity in his former position gives way to uncertainty in the conditions of his life. This is the sense of an old English proverb which says: he who speaks two languages is a knave. It is true that external and internal conflicts arise through the multiplicity of group-affiliations, which threaten the individual with psychological tensions or even a schizophrenic break. But it is also true that multiple group-affiliations can strengthen the individual and reenforce the integration of his personality. Conflicting and integrating tendencies are mutually reenforcing. Conflicting tendencies can arise just because the individual has a core of inner unity. The ego can become more clearly conscious of this unity, the more he is confronted with the task of reconciling within himself a diversity of group-interests. The effect of marriage on both spouses is that they belong to several families; this has always been a source of enrichment, a way of expanding one's interests and relationships but also of intensifying one's conflicts. These conflicts may induce the individual to make internal and external adjustments, but also to assert himself energetically.

In primitive clan-organizations the individual would participate in several groups in such a way that he belonged to the kinship or totemic group of his mother, but also to the narrower, familial or local association of his father. Now these simple people are not equal to conflicts such as those just mentioned, which is basically due to the fact that they lack a firm awareness of themselves as personalities. With peculiar purposefulness these two kinds of association are therefore so differently arranged that they do not encroach upon each other. Relationships on the maternal side have a more ideal, spiritual nature, whereas on the paternal side they are real, material and directly effective. In the case of the Australian aborigines, i.e., the Hereros, and among many other hunting tribes, maternal kinship, and similarly the totemic association, do not constitute a basis for community-living. They have no effect on daily life, but only on festive occasions of deep significance, such as marriage ceremonies and ceremonies occasioned by death and blood revenge. The last of these has an ideal, abstract character in the lives of the primitive peoples. The totemic association is transmitted through maternal descent and, therefore, it is often scattered through many tribes and hordes. It is held together only by common taboos on food and common ceremonials, and particularly by means of special names and special symbols on weapons. On the other hand, the paternal kinship-relations encompass all of daily life, waging war, alliances, inheritance, hunting, and so on. They do not have these taboos and symbols and do not need them, because the bond of a community in one locality and the convergence of their direct interests provide the basis for a sense of group-cohesion. At this stage, each connection which is not local usually assumes a more ideal character. It is the sign of a higher social development that group-cohesion can transcend local ties and yet be thoroughly realistic and concrete. But if the individual in a primitive tribe belongs to both the paternal-local group and to the maternal clan, these groups must be separated from each other in terms of the distinctly concrete or distinctly abstract values which they embody. Given the undifferentiated character of the primitive mind, this separation is a precondition for the possibility that the same individual belongs to both groups.

GROUP-AFFILIATIONS
AND THE FAMILY

THE CATHOLIC PRIESTHOOD represents examples of multiple group-affiliations which are unique in kind and also in the degree to which they were successful. No estate was excluded from the recruitment of priests and monks. The power of the ecclesiastical estate greatly attracted both the highest and the lowest social elements. In medieval England strong aversions between social classes prevailed generally. However, the priesthood, although it formed a strong and compact class, did not engender real class-hatred because it originated from all classes and every family had some relative who belonged to it. A similar situation was created by the fact that church-property existed everywhere. Because there was some church-property in every province and almost every community, alongside the infinite number of property titles characteristic of the Middle Ages, there arose an inter-regional uniformity of the clerical estate, which was both cause and consequence of its purposive unity. To date, this is the greatest example in history of the formation of a social group which cuts across all other existing groups. But at the same time it is characterized by the fact that it actually produced no overlapping of group-affiliations in the individuals. The priesthood could establish a relationship to, and could communicate with, all existing social strata in a manner which was entirely unbiased, because the individual priest was completely released from the ties with his social stratum; he was not even permitted to retain his name. Otherwise, these ties would have determined the personality of the priest together with those which he had newly gained in the priesthood.

But the personality of the priest was determined instead by his affiliation with the priesthood and the consequences of this situation confirm our analysis, albeit by means of a contradiction. The priest may possess no individuality in the normal sense, he cannot possess any traits which would differentiate him from other priests. Since he is entirely a priest, he must be a priest to the exclusion of all other concerns. Thus, the overlapping of group-affiliations has no effect upon the individual in this case, but only upon the estate as a whole, which is made up of *former* members of *all* estates and groups. That the priesthood as a higher social form was determined sociologically on the basis of overlapping group-affiliations, was possible only because the priesthood stood in the same relationship to all of the groups. Among the means utilized by Catholicism, celibacy is the most radical method by which the individual priest was put outside the network of group-affiliations.

Marriage constitutes a sociological determination of such finality that the individual is no longer quite free to attain a position in a group other than his family which would correspond to his interest in this second group. It is significant that the lower Russian clergyman, whose task demanded that he live among the people, is generally married, while the higher, ruling clergy are celibate. On the other hand, even the lowest ranking, Roman Catholic priest occupies in his village a somewhat abstract position which isolates him from the community-life of his environment. To be sure, the priesthood of the Russian Church is only an approximation of the Protestant clergy, which as a matter of principle is entirely enmeshed in civil life. The Russian priesthood is almost completely endogenous: priests of the Greek Orthodox Church seldom marry anyone other than the daughters of priests. Marriage is often so significant for the other sociological ties of the husband, that associations are actually differentiated on the basis of whether or not the marriage of their members are of consequence for these associations.

In the Middle Ages and even later the marriage of a journeyman was regarded with displeasure by his fellows. Indeed, in several associations of journeymen difficulties were placed in the way of a married journeyman who desired membership. For marriage restricted the migration of journeymen, which was essential not only for the unity and inner solidarity of the journeymen's estate, but also for the ready mobility of the group in accordance with shifting opportunities for work. The marriage of a journeyman ran counter also to the homogeneity of interest, the independence of the group in relation to their masters, and the social cohesion of the estate. Because of the peculiar structure of marriage and the family, the overlapping of group-affiliations inevitably resulted in this case in the rather extensive withdrawal of the individual from all social ties.

It is apparent that, for similar reasons, celibacy was considered appropriate for the soldier wherever a clearly differentiated military estate [officer corps] existed. However, in the Macedonian regiments of the Ptolemies and afterwards in the era of the Roman Emperors, soldiers were permitted to marry or to have concubines. [This distinction between officers and men is similar to the distinction between the higher and the lower Russian clergy.] The regiments were often replenished from among the offspring of these unions. Only the thoroughgoing fusion of the modern army with the structure of national life has completely abolished the rule of celibacy for the officers.

It is also plain that the same formal pattern of social relations may occur with reference to other conditions, even though this is not so striking and basic a case as that of marriage. The old scholastic universities refused to accept students [who were native residents of the town]. In the city of Bologna the rights of membership in the university were withdrawn from those students who acquired citizenship after a residence of more than ten years. In like manner, the Hanseatic League of German merchants in Flanders excluded every compatriot who had acquired Flemish citizenship.

As a rule an overlapping of group-affiliations cannot occur if the social groups involved are too far apart with regard to their purpose and in terms of the demands they make upon the individual. And a group which wants its members to become absorbed unconditionally in its activities must regard it as incompatible with this principle if an individual is differentiated from other members by virtue of his simultaneous affiliation with another group. Of course, the element of jealousy between groups enters in as well.

CROSS-PRESSURES ARISING FROM
MULTIPLE GROUP-AFFILIATIONS:
EXAMPLES FROM THE MIDDLE AGES

THE SOCIOLOGICAL DETERMINATION of the individual will be greater when the groups which influence him are juxtaposed than if they are concentric. That is to say, human aggregates such as the nation, a common social position, an occupation, and specific niches within the latter, do not allot any special position to the person who participates in them, because participation in the smallest of these groups already implies participation in the larger groups. But groups which are interrelated in this way do not always control individuals in a unified way. The fact that these associations are related to each other in a concentric way may mean not that they are related organically but that they are in mechanical juxtaposition. Hence, these associations will affect the individual, as if each of them was independent of the other.

This is manifest in earlier systems of law, when a person guilty of a crime is punished twice: by the immediate group to which he belongs and by the wider one which includes the first. If in late medieval Frankfurt a member of a guild had not fulfilled his obligation to render military service, he was punished by the head of his guild, but also by the city council. In a similar way, if in a libel suit the injured party had obtained satisfaction from the guild, it would still seek justice in the regular courts. And conversely, in the older guild systems the guild reserved the right to punish an offender, even though the court had already done so. This two-in-one type of procedure made it clear to the person affected by it that the two groups which enveloped him concentrically in a certain sense were also "intersecting" one another in his person. For his affiliation with the immediate group did not by any means comprise all the obligations which his affiliation with the larger group entailed. This is seen in the example cited above, in which the fact that a person belongs to a special category within a general occupational classification means that all those rules apply to him which apply to this general classification.

An antagonistic relationship between the immediate and the broader group has a special significance for the situation of the individual. This is shown in the following case.[3] If a larger group "A" consists of the smaller groups "m" and "n", it may happen that "A" is identical only with "m" in its immediate but essential implications, while "n" is in this respect opposed to "m". This was the relation between the free "Burgenses" or communities of townspeople and the Episcopal officials. In the early Middle Ages both groups together often made up the main body of a town's citizens; they actually constituted the city in the broad sense. But in the narrow sense only the townspeople proper were "the city." The officials and vassals of the episcopacy thus had a double position. They were members of the citizenry, and yet their interests and rights made them a part of quite different groups. Therefore, they were a part of the "Burgenses," on the one hand, but they stood in contrast to them, on the other. Their very position as vassals of the Bishop which alienated them from the town made them in every single case members of this particular town. If the townspeople were divided, for example, into guilds, then each individual was uniformly a member of this immediate group as well as of the broader community of the town. The Episcopal officials of the Bishop, however, were a part of the town-community, on the one hand, but they were differentiated from it, on the other. This relationship was so contradictory that later on the vassals either entered the community of townspeople proper or withdrew from it altogether.

Such awkwardness and difficulties arise for the person as a result of his affiliation with groups which surround him concentrically. Yet, this is one of the first and most direct ways in which the individual, who has begun his social existence by being affiliated with one group only, comes to participate in a number of groups. The peculiar character of group-formation in the Middle Ages in contrast with the modern

---

3. There are of course countless cases in which there is a general conflict between the whole and the part; these are not considered here.

way has been stressed frequently. In the Middle Ages affiliation with a group absorbed the whole man. It served not only a momentary purpose, which was defined objectively. It was rather an association of all who had combined for the sake of that purpose while the association absorbed the whole life of each of them. If the urge to form associations persisted, then it was accompanied by having whole associations combined in confederations of a higher order. This form, which enables the single individual to participate in a number of groups without alienating him from his affiliation with his original locality, may appear simple today, but it was in fact a great social invention. This form could be serviceable as long as men had not invented purposive associations, which made it possible for persons to work together by impersonal means for impersonal ends, and thereby to leave the personality of the individual inviolate. The enrichment of the individual as a social being which was attainable under the Medieval type of group-formation, was to be sure, a limited one, while the enrichment made possible by purposive associations is not limited in this sense.

Still, the enrichment under the Medieval type was considerable, for what the individual obtained from his affiliation with the larger group was in no way contained in the affiliation with his immediate group. By way of contrast, the concept "tree" of which the oak is a part, does contain all the elements of the concept "plant," which comprises the concept "tree" though much else besides. To subsume the oak under the concept "plant" entails a meaning for the oak, which is not revealed by subsuming "oak" under the concept "tree," however much the "tree" includes the conceptual elements of "plant" logically. This meaning is given by relating the oak to everything that is "plant" without being "tree." Much would have been gained in the medieval pattern of group-affiliation, even if nothing else had occurred than what is suggested by this analogy. The concentric pattern

of group-affiliations is a systematic and often also an historical stage, which is prior to that situation in which the groups
with which persons affiliate are juxtaposed and "intersect"
in one and the same person.

INDIVIDUALISM AND MULTIPLE
GROUP-AFFILIATION

THE MODERN PATTERN differs sharply from the concentric
pattern of group-affiliations as far as a person's achievements
are concerned. Today someone may belong, aside from his
occupational position, to a scientific association, he may sit
on a board of directors of a corporation and occupy an
honorific position in the city government. Such a person
will be more clearly determined sociologically, the less his
participation in one group by itself enjoins upon him participation in another. He is determined sociologically in the
sense that the groups "intersect" in his person by virtue of his
affiliation with them. Whether or not the fact that a person
who performs several functions reveals a characteristic combination of his talents, a special breadth of activity depends
not only on his participation in several offices and institutions
but naturally on the extent of their division of labor. In this
way, the objective structure of a society provides a framework within which an individual's non-interchangeable and
singular characteristics may develop and find expression, depending on the greater or lesser possibilities which that structure allows.

In England, it was long customary to staff a number of
quite different administrative bodies with the same personnel.
Already in the Middle Ages one and the same person could
be a circuit judge and a justice in Ireland, a member of the
Treasury and a Baron of the Exchequer, a member of the
King's court of justice and a Justice in Banco. As the same
group of persons formed so many different official boards,
it is apparent that none of these persons were especially char-

acterized by the mere fact of their participation on these boards. The objective functions of each person could not be differentiated sufficiently under these circumstances. And, therefore, his performance of several functions could not be an essential rationale of his individuality, nor could a knowledge of these functions provide a sufficient clue in this respect.

The individual may add affiliations with new groups to the single affiliation which has hitherto influenced him in a pervasive and one-sided manner. The mere fact that he does so is sufficient, quite apart from the nature of the groups involved, to give him a stronger awareness of individuality in general, and at least to counteract the tendency of taking his initial group's affiliations for granted. For this reason, representatives of the groups with which an individual is affiliated, are already opposed to the mere formality of a new affiliation, even if the purpose of the latter does not involve any competition with the previous group affiliations.

In the twelfth and thirteenth centuries the frequent imperial prohibitions of alliances between German towns were probably designed to meet real dangers. But in the Frankish, and at first also in the German, empire it was much more a matter of abstract principle that the government and the Church were opposed to the guilds. This was a case of an association based on free choice [guilds], the principle of which permitted an unlimited increase of associations; such associations were necessarily rivals of the powers exercised by existing associations. The mere fact of multiple group-affiliations enabled the person to achieve for himself an individualized situation in which the groups had to be oriented towards the individual. In the earlier situation the individual was wholly absorbed by, and remained oriented toward, the group.

Opportunities for individualization proliferate into infinity also because the same person can occupy positions of different rank in the various groups to which he belongs. This is already important with regard to familial relationships. The dissolution of the primitive Germanic class-organization was furthered greatly because consideration was given to the relatives of the wife as well as to all in-law relations. Thus one could belong to different kinship-groups at the same time. The rights and duties of each of these groups conflicted with those of every other so effectively that it has been said that only relatives existed but no kinship-associations. However, this result would not have come about, indeed the entire situation could not have arisen to this extent, if the individual had occupied the same position with regard to each line of relatives. But the individual occupied a central position in one group of relatives, while his position was peripheral in another; he had an authoritative position in the one group, but in the other his position made him the equal of many other relatives. In one situation the individual's economic interests would be involved, in another his involvement would be significant only in a personal sense. The structure of these connections excluded the possibility that a second individual would occupy exactly the same position within the same context.

Under these conditions of unilateral kinship the individual would have been born into a fixed position. And the accent of importance remained ever on the position which dominated the individual because kinship unilaterally determined that position. On the other hand, if the relations between kinship groups were multilateral, then it was the individual who brought about the contact of one line of relatives with another. Within the family such positions and their individual combinations could arise by themselves, as it were.

But each new group-formation produces immediately, and in a more deliberate way than the family, a certain inequality, a differentiation between the leaders and the led. If, as in the case of the humanists mentioned above, a common interest established a bond between persons of high and of low status, then this made inoperative such differences as divided them otherwise. Yet, new differences between high and low arose within this community of scholars according to criteria that were germane to it but that were out of keeping with the criteria of high and low, which prevailed in the other groups with which the humanists were affiliated. In this manner the personality of each individual was determined in a more characteristic and many-sided way than would be the case otherwise.

However, the same result can also be achieved, if equality prevails within a newly formed group, while its members occupy and retain positions of greatly varied rank in those groups with which they have been affiliated hitherto. Such a case is a highly significant sociological type in the sense that both the individual who ranks low in his original group and another who ranks high in his group, are now equals in a social sense. Medieval knighthood worked in this way, for example. Under its rules, the ministerial vassals of a Princely Court were members of an association of peers to which the prince, and even the emperor, belonged. All members of this association were equals in matters relating to the knighthood. This gave the ministerial vassal a position which had nothing to do with his duties of office, and rights which did not stem from his lord. The differences of birth between nobility, freemen, and vassals were not thereby eliminated. But these differences were "intersected" by a new line of division which was established by the association of all those who were bound together as equals in accordance with the rights and customs of knighthood. To be sure this association did not establish a real community but one which was effective through a common ideal; but as such this community maintained *one* standard of judgment for all. Any person, although he was affiliated with groups in which he stood either high or low, was at the same time part of a group in which he was the "equal" of every other. This was a combination of group-affiliation of a singular kind, which determined and enriched the vitality of the individual as a social being.

One and the same person may occupy positions of different rank in different groups. Since these positions are completely independent of one another, strange combinations of group-affiliations can arise. Thus, an intellectually and socially prominent man has to subordinate himself to a non-commissioned officer in countries with universal military training. Or take the beggar's guild in Paris which elects a "king," who was originally a beggar like all the others, and who, as far as I know, remains one, but who is given truly princely honors and privileges. This is perhaps the most remarkable and individualizing combination of low rank in one and high rank in another social position.

This overlapping may also take place within one and the same situation as soon as this includes a multiplicity of relationships—as for example in the case of the private tutor or even more so the earlier tutors of aristocratic youths. The tutor of princes is to be superior to his charge, he is to dominate and direct him—and yet he is, on the other hand, a servant, while his charge is the master. Another case: a corporal in Cromwell's army, who was well versed in the Bible, could deliver a moralizing sermon to his major, while he obeyed him without reservation in matters of military service. Finally, the content of these multiple relationships has decisive consequences for the individual the more they are a part of his personal life. There is, for example, the characteristic phenomenon of the aristocrat with liberal sentiments, of the man of the world who has distinctly religious tendencies, of the scholars, who seek their social contacts exclusively among men of affairs.

MULTIPLE GROUP-AFFILIATIONS
WITHIN A SINGLE GROUP

A TYPICAL EXAMPLE of multiple group-affiliations within a single group is the competition among persons who show their solidarity in other respects. On the one hand the merchant joins other merchants in a group which has a great number of common interests: legislation on issues of economic policy, the social prestige of business, representation of business-interests, joint action as over against the general public in order to maintain certain prices, and many others. All of these concern the world of commerce as such and make it appear to others as a unified group. On the other hand, each merchant is in competition with many others. To enter this occupation creates for him at one and the same time association and isolation, equalization and particularization. He pursues his interests by means of the most bitter competition with those with whom he must often unite closely for the sake of common interests. This inner contrast is probably most pronounced in the area of commerce, but it is present in some way in all other areas as well, down to the ephemeral socializing of an evening party.

An infinite range of individualizing combinations is made possible by the fact that the individual belongs to a multiplicity of groups, in which the relationship between competition and socialization varies greatly. It is a trivial observation that the instinctive needs of man prompt him to act in these mutually conflicting ways: he feels and acts *with* others but also *against* others. A certain measure of the one and the other, and a certain proportion between them, is a purely formal necessity for man, which he meets in the most manifold ways. Often this occurs in a manner, which makes an individual's action understandable not on the basis of its objective meanings, but on the basis of the satisfaction which it affords to the formal drives mentioned above. Individuality is characterized, both in regard to its natural striving and its historical development, by that proportion between socialization and competition which is decisive for it.

And the reverse tendency arises on the same basis: the individual's need for a clearer articulation and for a more unambiguous development of his personality, forces him to select certain groups. And from their combination he gains his maximum of individuality—the one group offering him opportunities for socialization, the other opportunities for competition. Thus, the members of a group in which keen competition prevails will gladly seek out such other groups as are lacking in competition as much as possible. As a result businessmen have a decided preference for social clubs. The estate-consciousness of the aristocrat, on the other hand, rather excludes competition within his own circle; hence, it makes supplementations of that sort [i.e., social clubs] largely superfluous. This suggests forms of socialization to the aristocrat which contain stronger competitive elements—for example, those clubs which are held together by a common interest in sports.

Finally, I shall mention here the frequent discrepancies which arise because an individual or a group are controlled by interests that are opposed to each other. This may permit individuals and groups to belong at the same time to parties which are opposed to each other. Individuals are likely to become affiliated with conflicting groups, if in a many-sided culture the political parties are intensely active. Under such conditions it usually happens that the political parties also represent the different viewpoints on those questions which have nothing at all to do with politics. Thus, a certain tendency in literature, art, religion, etc., is associated with one party, an opposite tendency with another. The dividing line which separates the parties is, thereby, extended throughout the entire range of human interests. Obviously, an individual who will not surrender completely to the dictates of the party, will join a group, say on the basis of his esthetic or religious convictions, which is amalgamated with his political enemies. He will be affiliated with two groups which regard each other as opponents.

RELIGION AS A FACTOR
IN MULTIPLE GROUP-AFFILIATIONS

RELIGIOUS AFFILIATION is the most important and at the same time the most characteristic example [of individualization] ever since religion has been emancipated from racial, national, or local ties, a world-historical fact of immeasurable significance. Either the religious community embraces the civic community in terms of its other essential or comprehensive interests, or the religious community is entirely free of all solidarity with whatever is *not* religion. The nature of religion is completely expressed in both of these sociological types, though in a different language or at another level of development in each case.

It is understandable that the co-existence and the sharing of human interests is not possible with people who do not share one's faith. The deeply justified need for unity was satisfied, *a priori* so to speak, in all of ancient civilization, in the Semitic as well as the Graeco-Roman world. Religion was made an affair of the tribe or the state. With a few exceptions, the deity was identified with the interests of the political group, and the duties toward Him were identical with the all-embracing duties toward the latter.

Yet the power of religious motivation is equally apparent, where it is independent of all social ties originating from other motives, and where it is strong enough to bring together believers adhering to the same creed, in spite of all the differences between them which arise out of their other affiliations. This form of religious organization is obviously a highly individualistic one. The religious temper has lost the support which it had obtained from its integration with the entire complex of social ties. Now religious experience is based upon the soul of the individual and it is his responsibility; on that basis the individual seeks to establish a bond with others who are similarly qualified in terms of their religious experience, but perhaps in no other respect. Christianity in its pure sense is an entirely individualistic religion, and this has made possible its diffusion throughout the manifold of national and local groups.[4] The Christian was conscious of the fact that he took with him his church-affiliation into every community of his choosing, regardless of the psychological influences and the duties which such a community exerted and made incumbent upon him. This consciousness must have created a feeling of individual determination and self-confidence.

This sociological significance of religion reflects its dual relationship to life. On the one hand, religion stands in contrast to the whole substance of human life; it is the counterpart and the equivalent of life itself, aloof from its secular movements and interests. On the other hand, religion takes sides among the parties in the secular life, though it had elevated itself above the world of affairs as a matter of principle. As such religion is an element of secular life alongside all its other elements; it becomes involved in the multitude of changing relationships though at the same time it rejects this involvement. As a result a remarkable involution occurs. The disavowal of all social ties, which is evidence of a deep religiosity, allows the individual and his religious group to come in contact with any number of other groups with whose members they do not share any common interests. And the relationships again serve to distinguish and to determine the individuals concerned as well as the religious groups.

This pattern is repeated in many specific religious situa-

---

4. In this respect Christianity is surpassed only by Buddhism in its original form, although Buddhism is not a religion in the real sense of that word, since it teaches that salvation can be won only in an absolutely personal way, without any transcendental mediation.

tions and in the peculiar intertwining between the religious and the other interests of individuals. In the quarrels between France and Spain, the Huguenots placed themselves at one time at the service of the king, when the struggles turned against Catholic Spain and its friends in France. On another occasion, when they were oppressed by the king, they joined Spain directly. The cruel suppression of the Irish Catholics by England revealed a dual position of another type. One day the Protestants of England and Ireland would feel united against a common religious enemy without regard for their fellow countrymen; the next day the Protestants and Catholics of Ireland would be united against the suppressor of their common fatherland without consideration of religious differences. By way of contrast the European states intervened in Asia to defend Chinese or Turkish Christians; but this action seemed quite outrageous and incomprehensible to people like the Chinese, among whom the primitive identity of religious and political group-affiliation is still unbroken.

But where this unity has been broken as much as in Switzerland, the abstract nature of religion—which because of this abstract quality occupies a definite position in relation to all other interests—brings about immediately very characteristic patterns of group-affiliation. Because of the enormous differences between its cantons, Switzerland does not have a system of political parties such that politically like-minded people in the various cantons would divide themselves into major parties with regard to the national government. Only the *ultramontane people of all cantons*, [i.e., Catholics who follow the Papal authority in all questions of secular and ecclesiastical policy] form a joint group in political affairs.

One can assume without question that this emancipation of religious from political ties has also consequences in the opposite direction, in that it will make possible political mergers which would have been frustrated by the continuing unity of both. The most striking example is perhaps the union between Scotland and England in 1707. For both countries the advantages of becoming a *single* state were bound up with the continued existence of the two churches. Up to that time political and religious concepts had been closely inter-related in both countries. Only the separation of Church and State made the amalgamation of political interests between the two countries possible; otherwise the ecclesiastical inter-ests would not have tolerated it. It was said of the two coun-tries that they could preserve harmony only by agreeing to differ. Once this solution, together with its consequences for group-affiliation, had taken place, then it was no longer pos-sible to abolish the freedom which had been gained. Hence the principle: *cuius regio eius religio*, is valid only if it does not need to be stated explicitly, but instead reflects the ex-istence of a naive and undifferentiated condition in which Church and State are at one.

It is quite remarkable when the religious point of view overcomes all other bases of separation and amalgamates per-sons and interests despite their natural differentiation. Yet, this religious unity is thought of as quite parallel to those [other cases of organized solidarity] which arise merely on the basis of an objective differentiation. Thus in 1896 the Jewish workers of Manchester came together in an organi-zation which was to include *all* categories of workers (mainly these were tailors, shoemakers, and bakers) and which in-tended to make common cause with the other trade unions in regard to the interests of labor. But the other trade unions were organized in accordance with the *objective* differences between types of work. This principle of organization was so important that the Trade Unions could not be induced to amalgamate with the International, because the latter was constituted without regard for the type of work in which its members were engaged. Although the case of the Jewish workers seems to go back to the undifferentiated community of interests in the religious as well as the social and economic sense, it reveals nevertheless the separation of these interests, at least on principle. The voluntary coordination of the Jewish workers with trade-unions organized on a purely objective basis [namely the division of labor] reveals that their organization was based on a practical purpose [rather than in accordance with religious belief].

The situation is manifestly different in the case of the Catholic trade unions of Germany, because of their great scope, because of the political significance of Catholicism in Germany, and because their religion does not place the Catholic workers in as conspicuous a position as the Jewish workers, (For example, in Germany the religious differentiation has produced special workers' associations within the general Catholic organizations. In Aachen a number of years ago, weavers, spinners, finishers, needlemakers, metal workers and construction workers were organized in this way.) Catholic organizations are large enough to allow for this division without involving an overlapping of group-affiliations such that each of these special associations would join with non-Catholic workers in the same trade. Still, this latter development has already occurred on occasion and that inner division is apparently the first step in this direction.

PRIESTHOOD AS A SPECIAL TYPE
OF GROUP-FORMATION

FINALLY there arise overlapping group-affiliations on a higher level, in that religious forces become sublimated in the priesthood. The relationship between believers and priests involves representation and leadership, control and cooperation, veneration and the provision of material sustenance. To be sure, the sociological form of this relationship varies in some respects with each religion. But the relations between believers and priests have so much in common that one can, with reservations, speak of a formally similar position of the priest within groups, however much these differ in all other respects.[5] Out of this there arises above all a solidarity of interests, a mutual understanding, a cohesiveness among the priests, which under certain conditions can even drown out the substantive antagonism between Evangelical ministers and Catholic priests.

A single priest or a kindred group of priests belong both to a national, a denominational, and in some sense a party-like association, and to that association of all clergies which arises partly from a sociological and partly from an ethical-metaphysical kinship. This overlapping of group-affiliations gives to the individual priest a peculiarly determined character which sets him apart from other members of the one group as well as of the other. [Simmel refers here to the contrast between the priest and the believers as a group within one church, and to the contrast between the priests of all churches and all believers.]

INDIVIDUALISM AND COLLECTIVISM IN MODERN SOCIETY

THE DEVELOPMENT of the public mind shows itself by the fact that a sufficient number of groups is present which have form and organization. Their number is sufficient in the sense that they give an individual of many gifts the opportunity to pursue each of his interests in association with others. Such multiplicity of groups implies that the ideals of collectivism and of individualism are approximated to the same extent. On the one hand the individual finds a community for each of his inclinations and strivings which makes it easier to satisfy them. This community provides an organizational form for his activities, and it offers in this way all the advantages of group-membership as well as of organizational experience. On the other hand, the specific qualities of the individual are preserved through the combination of

---

5. In the same way we may speak of the formally similar position of the nobleman, the warrior, the merchant.

groups which can be a different combination in each case.

Thus one can say that society arises from the individual and that the individual arises out of association. An advanced culture broadens more and more the social groups to which we belong with our whole personality; but at the same time the individual is made to rely on his own resources to a greater extent and he is deprived of many supports and advantages associated with the tightly-knit, primary group. Thus, the creation of groups and associations in which any number of people can come together on the basis of their interest in a common purpose, compensates for that isolation of the personality which develops out of breaking away from the narrow confines of earlier circumstances.

GROUP-FORMATION
AND THE "CODE OF HONOR"

THE EXTENT to which associations [based on interest] also form a tightly-knit group may be gauged on the basis of whether and to what extent such a group has developed a special code of "honor." Such a code would imply that every member of the group would feel that his honor was diminished whenever any member suffered an insult or a deprivation of his honor. In this sense the association possesses a collective sense of honor, whose changes are reflected in the sense of honor of each member. Groups make certain that the conduct of their members will be appropriate through the establishment of a specific concept of honor, such as family-honor, the honor of an officer, the reputation of a businessman for honest dealing. They do so especially with regard to those specific differences which mark them off from the broadest social group [the state]. It should be remembered that the public laws which regulate the conduct of individuals towards the state under the threat of coercion contain no stipulation concerning their conduct within the group. A single person may be affiliated with a number of particular groups, which create specific codes of honor. The broader group [such as the state] develops a concept of honor which is valid for the members of special groups. But this broad concept is more abstract, more general than, and in this sense different from, the particularistic concepts of honor of the special groups.

Hence, criteria of honor in all their intricacies become the symbols of social groups. Status-honor even exists in the negative sense. This status-dishonor, so to speak, allows for a certain latitude of behavior, which is regarded as human enough or even as honorable in the entire society. This negative code permits deviation from, just as the positive code of honor adds demands [to, what is already generally expected]. Thus, many categories of tradesmen and especially speculators but also the Penny-a-Liner [hackwriter] and the Demi-Monde were permitted to do certain things which would not be regarded generally as honorable, but in which they were protected by a good conscience derived from an established code of conduct. However, alongside this conventional form of dishonorable conduct, the individual can be quite honorable in the established sense of the word in his general human relationships, just as the adherence to a specific code of honor does not prevent the individual from behaving on the side in a way that would be considered quite dishonorable by generally accepted criteria. Thus, different aspects of the individual can be subsumed under different codes of honor which reflect the different groups to which the person belongs simultaneously.

As a result, the same demand can receive two emphases which are quite different. It may be the maxim of an individual not to suffer insults in silence, but he will act on this maxim in private life one way, and in quite a different manner as a reserve officer or as an incumbent of an official position. Respect for women as a means to maintain one's own masculine honor will have its characteristic emphasis in a pastor's family and a different one in a group of young lieutenants. Hence, a member of the latter group who comes from a pastor's family, can perceive clearly his membership in both groups through his experience of the conflict between these two concepts of honor.

Generally, this elaboration of special codes of honor for different status-groups reveals one of the most important, formal-sociological developments. It manifests itself a thousandfold in a wholly rudimentary manner, in mere nuances of feeling and acting, and often disguised by motives of a more personal or more materialistic kind. The narrowly circumscribed and strict custom of earlier conditions was one in which the social group as a whole, i.e., its central governing body, regulated the conduct of the individual in the most varied ways. Since then, the group has limited its regulations more and more to the basic interests of the general public. By the same token the individual has gained more and more spheres of freedom for himself. These spheres of freedom are then preempted by new group-formations, but in such a way that the individual determines on the basis of his interests to which group he wants to belong.

As a consequence the feeling of honor suffices, in lieu of external methods of coercion, to make the individual conform to those norms which are required for the stability of the group. Moreover, this process does not originate solely from the coercive power of government. Group-sanctions originally control the several aspects of an individual's interests, and these interests are essentially unrelated to the purposes of the sanctions. But in the end the individual is left to pursue his interests by joining with others in special associations, in which participation is a matter of personal choice. Such a development occurs also in the family, in the guild, in the religious community, etc. The problem of socialization can be solved in these special associations in a much more adequate way than in the earlier, more confining groups which neglected the concerns of the individual.

PATTERNS OF FREEDOM AND OBLIGATION

NO MATTER how extensive, severe and all pervasive the control of group-sanctions over the individual may be, there will remain some relationships in his life which will escape it. These relationships will be left in a careless and aimless way to the pure arbitrariness of the individual, the more so, in fact, the more the remaining relationships are subject to coercion. Accordingly, the Greek citizen, but still more the citizen of ancient Rome, had to submit unconditionally to the norms and purposes of his national community in all matters connected in any way with politics. But as the master of his home he exercised an autocratic rule which was just as unconditional. Similarly, the close social cohesion which we observe in small primitive tribes, permits its individual members a complete freedom to behave in any way they please toward persons not belonging to the tribe. Again, tyranny is correlated with, and indeed supports, the most perfect freedom and an utter abandon of all restraint in those personal relations which have no importance to its own purposes. This is an inexpedient distribution of collective coercion and individual arbitrariness.

It is more appropriate and just, if objective facts and personal interests determine the form and the purpose of voluntary associations. In that case the activities which were previously uncontrolled and wholly determined by the individual will find a collectivist form. For the individual seeks to establish social contacts with regard to his several interests to the extent that he is liberated [from coercive sanctions]. And he will limit his arbitrariness voluntarily, since it is but a compensatory substitute for being wholly determined by collective sanctions. Thus we find an especially strong development of club life[6] in countries with great political freedom. And we find a lively development of sects in those religious communities which are without an ecclesiastic power of strong hierarchical tendencies. In short, freedom and obligation are more evenly distributed, if the process of socialization allows for the possibility that homogeneous individuals come together from heterogeneous groups rather than compel the heterogeneous components of the individual to be [accommodated to the uniform demands] of one group.

MECHANICAL AND FUNCTIONAL CRITERIA AS PRINCIPLES OF ORGANIZATION IN ADMINISTRATION, MEDICINE, TRADE, AND CONSUMERS' COOPERATIVES

ONE OF the most important forms of a progressive development may be characterized as follows. The differentiation and division of labor is at first of a quantitative nature so to speak. Spheres of activity are divided in such a fashion that an individual, or a group, may be engaged in different activities, and each sphere of activity comprises a number of qualitatively different relations. However, later on these differences are distinguished and segregated, and like elements from all of the groups are now integrated in one qualitatively uniform activity.

In the development of public administration we frequently

---

6. Of course, this club life may also develop on a different political basis, for instance, where decidedly individualistic tendencies clash with an extensive governmental tutelage. In this case, the emphasis is placed especially on the individualistic element in the formation of clubs, on the amount of freedom which is embodied in such clubs as over against governmental regulation. This provides the individual with organizational support against the state. Here, as in the case mentioned in the text, the consciousness of freedom and of obligation join on a sociological basis. But in the example in the text, the consciousness of freedom pertains to the political grouping, the consciousness of obligation to the club. Here it is the other way around. The same holds true for the second example in the text.

find that at first the center of government lacks all differentiation. Only later on, a series of functions are distinguished, such that each is controlled either by a single person or a single administrative authority. However, these administrative functions are at first limited to a restricted local area. For example, the French National Council sends an "Intendant" into a province in order to exercise there all of the different functions which are otherwise exercised by the Council itself in the whole country. This division of labor is based on local areas according to the amount of work involved.

The later development of a division of functions differs from this geographic division, as, for instance, in the case of various ministries which develop out of the National Council. The activity of each of these ministries extends over the entire country, but only with regard to one function which is qualitatively distinct from others. The system of promotion of civil services employees which applies throughout the country, corresponds to this process. This nation-wide system has two advantageous features as contrasted with promotions limited to one geographic area. It makes it possible for an official to be transferred with relative ease to a position which is most suitable for him in terms of his ability and merits. And the system promotes more intimate reciprocal relations among the sections of the country with regard to each function of government. Therefore, only transfers of higher civil servants answer the purpose, while as a rule subordinate officials remain in the same sphere of activity all their lives. Hence, personal talent is of greater importance in the higher civil servant than in the routine activity of the subordinate. And this personal talent is both cause and effect of the changing interaction between his official functions and the trends and interests of many different localities. The degree of freedom evident in this network of overlapping group-affiliations [of the higher civil servant in France] is greater than it would be in an assignment fixed to a specific locality. This greater degree of freedom has its analogue in the life of the individual as we have seen.

Now we must consider a phenomenon which seems to contradict the differentiation just shown in the illustration from France. But in reality this does represent the same phenomenon on a higher level. During the Directory[7] each government department was controlled almost independently, the Legal Branch by Rewbell, the Police by Barras, the War Department by Carnot, etc. However, a completely different division of functions existed for the appointment of civil servants in the provinces. Here, Rewbell administered the East, Barras the South, Carnot the North, etc. Hence, the differentiation of administrative functions was preserved in accordance with objective criteria, which cut across all local differences. However, in appointing civil servants, technical competence was actually only a secondary requirement. More important was knowledge of the local area and personnel. In this case, the procedure of a regional division of functions, which cut across all varieties of technical competence, was the suitable one.

A contrasting illustration is shown by the remarkable lack of differentiation of the Consejos, advisory ministries, which were formed under Philipp II of Spain. According to an Italian report, there were the following ministries: dell'Indie, di Castiglia, d'Aragona, d'inquisizione, di camera, dell'ordini, di guerra, di hazzienda, di giustizia, d'Italia, di stato. Since all of these seem to have been co-ordinated, the activities of the technical ministers and those of the regional ministers must have been in incessant collision. Here we have a division of functions as such, so to speak, based on no principle at all, because the regional division and the division by subject matter are made equally effective *without* differentiation.

---

7. The period from 1795 to 1799 when five men constituted the executive of the French government. (R.B.)

In ancient Egypt specialization in medicine required a different training for those physicians treating the arm from those treating the leg. This, then, was also a "local" differentiation in terms of parts of the body. Unlike this practice, modern medicine entrusts the same pathological conditions, no matter on what part of the body they occur, to the same specialist, so that again functional identity prevails in what is treated together, rather than accidental external criteria. This criterion of functional identity is reversed—though in a different aspect—in the case of those specialists who treat all ailments rather than special ailments only, but who do so only by one special method or remedy. Practitioners, for example, who cure everything exclusively with water. Here we notice the same one-sidedness as in the case of the Egyptian physicians, only that—thanks to modern developments—it is of a functional rather than "local" character.

This proves that even when things are grouped together according to functional criteria, there still remains the difference between a method which uses external mechanical criteria and one which employs criteria that are appropriate in objective terms. For example, modern methods of distribution are illustrated by stores carrying different items for the production of complicated objects—as for instance, all supplies for railroads, all articles for restaurateurs, for dentists, shoemakers, warehouses for all household and kitchen furnishings, etc. These new methods of distribution supersede older methods which differentiated between items and grouped them together according to mechanical criteria. The consistent viewpoint according to which items obtained from the most varied sources of production are here assembled, consists in their relation to a common purpose which all of them serve, *terminus ad quem*. In most other cases, the division of labor is organized in terms of the uniformity in the method of production, *terminus a quo*. Stores which assemble commodities with regard to one common purpose, presuppose others that do so with regard to their common source of production. The first type represents an accentuated form of the division of labor by bringing together parts from entirely heterogeneous branches of production, each of which operates on the basis of a detailed division of labor. To bring together diverse parts in accordance with one viewpoint means, figuratively speaking, that a new key brings various parts in harmony with each other.

Finally, the consumer's cooperatives represent another, entirely different case in which group-formation depends on objective considerations which are combined with others that are logically incompatible with them. This holds true especially for those cooperatives established for definite occupational categories: for laborers, army-officers, civil servants. The goods carried in cooperatives for officers and civil servants are—with a few exceptions—the same. It is a pure formality, independent of all substantive considerations, which keeps the cooperatives for these two groups separated. Yet, the practical purpose involved is this: the department store for German civil servants is a joint stock company which has the same relations with its customers as any privately owned store. The more people buy there, the better this serves its purpose; restriction to a special group of customers would not be a requirement necessary for its successful operation. Yet, if it had been run simply as a cooperative store serving everybody, or as an ordinary store selling reliably at standard prices, it certainly would have lagged far behind the success which was actually attained. It was in fact this restriction of customers to a particular group which obviated difficulties and uncertainties usually incurred in ordinary business, though the restriction was entirely unnecessary on any substantive grounds. This restriction has a strong appeal to all those included in the group of customers, if for no other reason than that it excludes all others. All these facts—except perhaps this last one—have in themselves no apparent sociological significance. They serve here only as analogies of sociological combinations and developments and as such they illustrate that the latter conform to formal and normative patterns, which prevail generally far beyond the field of sociology.

THE SIGNIFICANCE OF CONCEPTS
IN THE FORMATION OF GROUPS

THE UNITY OF OBJECTS in accordance with external, mechanical criteria, the differentiation of objects, the synthesis of elements on rational and substantive grounds, the construction of new configurations from a higher and more comprehensive point of view—all these are typical forms of the human intellect. Sociological patterns are revealed in social life in an unlimited number of ways, but these patterns themselves are emanations of more general and deeply seated psychological functions. Throughout, form and content are but relative concepts. They are categories of knowledge to master the phenomena, and to organize them intellectually, so that the same thing which in any one relation, as though looked at from above, appears as form, must be labelled "content" in another relation, as though looked at from below.

The solidarity of wage labor exemplifies a group-formation based on a pervasive social awareness. This social consciousness is especially interesting because it presupposes a high degree of abstraction over and above the particularities of individuals and of groups. No matter what the job of the individual worker may be, whether he makes cannons or toys, the very fact that he is working for wages makes him join the group of those who are paid in the same way. The workers' identical relation to capital constitutes the decisive factor, i.e. wage labor is in a similar condition in the most diversified activities and all those are organized who find themselves in this condition.

There is immense significance in the psychological differentiation, by which the collective concept "laborer" evolved from such concepts as weavers, mechanics, miners, etc. This was already recognized by the English Conservatives at the beginning of the nineteenth century. By means of the Corresponding Societies Act, they succeeded in prohibiting all written communication among workers' associations as well as among all societies whose membership was composed of people from different trades. Evidently, the Conservatives were well aware that in this way a new social stratum would be created and that unpredictable complications would arise from the relations between this new stratum and the older ones. This new social stratum would be established, 1. if the general pattern of labor-relations was once severed from its fusion with each special trade; 2. if the association of a number of trades would emphasize those interests common to all workers and thereby paralyze the divisive effects of the differences existing between them.

After the various trades have developed out of the growing division of labor, more abstract considerations now cut across the differences between the trades and establish a new social group on the basis of what the trades have in common. Here, logical and socio-historical processes act and react on one another. To achieve this result, industry had to develop to such an extent, that hundreds or thousands of workers were subject to identical working conditions and that the interdependence of the different trades would grow along with the increasing division of labor. A money-economy had to become all-pervasive so that the value of the individual's performance would be reduced entirely to its monetary equivalent. Finally, demands for a high standard of living had to increase out of proportion to the level of wages. All these developments are the conditions which give a decisive significance to the role of labor in society.

These social forces and relationships come to a focus in the general concept of the "wage laborer," and the "wage laborer" is in turn a source of influences, which is based on the fact that workers have joined associations according to logical or formal criteria of like interests. As was mentioned above, the International Workingmen's Association had formed its sections at first without regard for the differences between trades. Later on this was changed and the sections were formed on the basis of the trade unions. Yet, this change was merely a formal organizational device which was believed to be more conducive to the general interest of workers. The guiding consideration of this policy was still the idea of "workers as such." This idea obliterated conceptually all the different types of labor, and this merely logical notion has assumed juridical significance. Safety measures, accident-insurance and their attendant rights have created a juridical concept of the worker and have given it substantive meaning, so that the mere fact that someone is a worker, has by itself certain legal consequences.

Moreover, there were purely factual consequences in addition to the logical, ethical, juridical implications of the fact that workers were regarded as such irrespective of all the differences between them. Only this made a "general strike" possible, since such a strike would not serve the purpose of a single trade, but would be called in order to force through a recognition of political rights for labor as a whole, as did, for example, the strike of the Chartists in 1842, or the Belgian strike of 1893. It is interesting to observe how this concept, once it had become a general idea, retained this general character and had the same consequences, even in smaller aggregations.

In France, there has been a law concerning professional and trade associations since 1884 according to which twenty or more persons of the *same* or related occupations may constitute themselves as a syndicate without a license from the government. Soon after, a syndicate of "railroad workers" was founded, whose members did not in fact pursue the same occupation. The common factor among all these smiths and porters, switchmen and saddlers, conductors and mechanics was exclusively that they were all workers in the employ of the railroad. The purpose of forming such a syndicate was, of course, that in this way the individual occupation could put pressure on the management, for which the isolated strength of each group would not have sufficed. The general concept of the "worker" has been given a narrower meaning: the general concept of the "railroad worker." In this case a logical procedure has been used to eliminate all the specialized types of railroad-work and the general concept of the "railroad worker" has become by the same token an immediately practical matter.

The form in which the broader concept of "the worker" brings about the same result usually involves a coalition of coalitions. In this case, the initial association has already eliminated all personal elements and the abstract concept of the carpenter or the shoemaker, of the glassblower or the weaver prevails. But once a coalition of such associations takes place, then the abstract concept of "the worker" stands out because all substantive differences between different types of work are ruled out as a matter of principle. The mason as such does not care, of course, whether the calico printer, who belongs to the same trade union federation, gets higher or lower hourly wages. Hence, the purpose of the federation is to obtain more favorable working conditions not for the individual worker but for labor as a whole.

The Solidarity of Employers. Similar relations occur when employers in different types of business form a coalition. The employer in one type of business is essentially indifferent towards the employer-employee relations in another. The aim of the coalition is only to strengthen the position of employers as a whole as opposed to labor as a whole. The general concept of "the entrepreneur" must arise as a correlate to that of labor. But this logical simultaneity does not have an immediate psychological and practical equivalent. This is probably due to three reasons: 1. the smaller number of employers as compared to the number of workers; the larger the number of a given kind are involved, the more readily a general concept is formed; 2. the competition of employers among each other, which does not exist among the workers; and 3. the identification of entrepreneurial activity in each case with its own field of endeavor, an identification which has been mitigated only in recent times in the course of capitalist development.

Modern industrial technique renders the worker much more indifferent to his specific type of work than the employer to his factory. That is the reason why for the worker the connection with all his fellow workers is more obvious, regardless of specialization, than is true in the parallel case of the employer and his connection with his fellow employers. In the end, the solidarity of labor had nevertheless the effect of creating in many respects a solidarity of employers and of giving rise thereby to a general concept of "the entrepreneur."

Coalitions of employers were formed not only in the same type of business; federations were also formed on the basis of employer-associations in different types of business. Already in 1892 an association of employers was formed in the United States in view of the strikes of workers which were getting out of hand. This association of employers was designed to oppose labor with party-like solidarity and resistance. At an earlier time, there had existed an essential solidarity between employer and employee, despite many disputes between them. This solidarity had been based on the identification of both with the productive activity itself. But the general concepts of "the worker" and "the entrepreneur" have cut across each particular pattern of employer-employee relations. Thereby, general concepts have gained preponderance over the solidarity between employer and employee which had formerly existed. In lieu of this solidarity we now have the relation of two general, abstract concepts, and the conflict between them seems logically predetermined. The individual worker and the individual employer represent merely accidental examples of the general concepts, and the substantive ties between them, which were based on their common interest in the work, are receding.

The Solidarity of the Mercantile Class. Sociologically the genesis of the mercantile class is related to that of the laboring class. Based partly on concrete and partly on abstract considerations, the mercantile class is a combination of persons, each of whom is only a merchant in general no matter what he sells. However, in this case it is relatively easy to detach the general from the specific, because the function of the individual salesman is such that the form of his activity is largely independent from its substance. The difference between the activity of the worker and of the salesman may be stated as follows. The activity of the worker depends entirely on what he does; hence it is difficult to separate the concept of his activity from the nature of his work. The activity of the salesman, on the other hand, is relatively independent of the items with which he deals. Especially in primitive conditions a great variety and an unpredictable change of objects may all be involved in the same functions of purchasing, peddling and finding buyers. Originally there is reference to "the merchant" as such. To this day, we frequently find storesigns in small German towns with the inscription "Merchandise" without further indication of the kind of goods sold in the store.

These functional characteristics of the individual merchant are again the characteristics of the great number of businessmen in a developed economy. The variety of commodities is divided among the special branches of commerce. This allows the common element in all commercial dealings to become the logical tie of the mercantile class, since these dealings are not intimately tied up with each type of business in any case. This community of interest is embodied in a concept [the mercantile class] which cuts across all the differences between types of business. And the barriers between businessmen which had existed apart from the differences of goods in which they traded were also broken down by the concept of the mercantile class.

Until the beginning of our modern era the individual foreign "nations" possessed specific privileges in the important commercial centers. These privileges demarcated them from one another, and from the residents as well, and caused each to establish itself as a special group. In the sixteenth century, however, when free trade was granted in Antwerp and Lyon, the merchants came together in large numbers unfettered by the conflicts and the segregation arising from these privileges. Coincident with this unprecedented concentration of commercial traffic, a general "mercantile class" was formed from among the individuals of the former "nations." Now the rights and usages were similar for all members of the mercantile class; they were no longer affected by differences between types of business or by differences arising from individual and national peculiarities. Even now one can observe that the rules governing commercial transactions become more clearly separated from the stipulations required for any one type of transaction, as the subdivisions of a given branch of production increase in number. On the other hand, in places essentially devoted to one branch of industry, we find that the concept "industrialist" is still identified implicitly with the local specialty of production, as in the case of the iron-magnate, the clothing or the toy-manufacturer. In one-industry towns the customary practices of other fields of business and of industrial transactions in general will be borrowed from that brance of production of which people are most conscious.

In this case, too, experience is in keeping throughout with the psychology of logical reasoning: if there was only one species of trees, the concept "tree" would never have been created. In the same way, it is the highly discriminating person of catholic training and activities who tends to have cosmopolitan reactions and convictions; one-sided people perceive what is human only in terms of their own limited horizon, since they are lacking in empathy for people different from themselves and are unable to experience vicariously what is common to all men. As has been mentioned, the practical consequences of the formation of higher generalities [concepts, associations, etc.] need not always occur in chronological order; frequently these generalities may, in turn, provide the stimulus, which helps to create a consciousness of social solidarity. Thus, the solidarity of craftsmen is promoted, for example, by the system of apprenticeship. The wages and the quality of labor may be reduced by an excessive employment of apprentices. But remedial action against this abuse in one craft would have the effect that the apprentices would be pushed out of one trade only to over-crowd another. This proves that only united action can help. And united action is possible only when there is a variety of crafts at the same time that a consciousness of the unity of all the craft-trades arises, which transcends the specific differences between them.

The Solidarity of Women. Finally I mention a fourth example[8] in addition to those of labor, the employers and the mercantile class. This example illustrates the segregation of a more or less abstract group, whose general conceptual elements had been associated closely with the separate affiliations of each group-member. Because of this conceptual segregation these members constitute a new social group. But they now stand at the "crossroads" between this new affiliation and the old ties, which remain from the time when each

---

8. Simmel actually speaks of the *third* example. But his treatment differentiates between employers of labor and merchants, in addition to his discussion of labor. Therefore I call the following discussion of women a "fourth example." (R.B.)

member was confined to a single group. I am referring to the social development of the concept "woman" in recent times. This development enables us to observe a number of complex formal patterns, not easily observed otherwise.

Up to now the sociological position of the individual woman had certain peculiar elements. The most general of her qualities, the fact that she was a woman and as such served the functions proper to her sex, caused her to be classified with all other women under one general concept. It was exactly this circumstance which removed her from the processes of group-formation in their strict sense, as well as from all actual solidarity with other women. Because of her peculiar functions she was relegated to activities within the limits of her home, confined to devote herself to a single individual, and prevented from transcending the group-relations established by marriage, family, social life, and perhaps charity and religion. The parallelism in the way of life and the activities of women is of such a nature as to effectively prevent the development of associations on the basis of this equality. This is the case, because each woman is so totally preoccupied in her own sphere that another, equally situated woman is by the same token totally excluded. In this way, her general qualification as a woman is from the outset the fundamental reason why she will become an integral part of her home and its range of interests. This is in utmost sociological contrast to the salesman, for example, whose activity is almost automatically divided into general form and special contents, as we have been above. In very primitive ethnological conditions women appear to be less dissociated and act on occasion as a unified party in opposition to the men. In these cases the woman probably has not yet become absorbed so completely by domestic interests as she has in the more highly developed epochs. However tyrannical the domination of the man may be, these simpler and less differentiated conditions of family and home do not lead her as far away from the general feminine interests, shared by all women, as does the cultured home which absorbs all her energies in this one particular network of obligations.

In our time it is sociologically very characteristic that this network of obligations has become less stringent and the problem of the emancipation of women has arisen. This problem has become a common concern of women as a group which has led to all sorts of actions, changes of conditions, and to the formation of groups. Isolation of women from one another, caused by the integration of each into an entirely individual sphere, was based upon the complete differentiation of women from men. As a result of our culture, man appears on the whole to be the higher type in terms of the training of intellect and the development of activity, in terms of self-assertion and the ability to relate to the environment. Even apart from questions of ranking, the two sexes appear to be so essentially different, that they can only be destined to complement one another. The meaning of feminine existence lies exclusively in what the man cannot be or do, or does not want to be or do. Consequently, this meaning of the life of women does not refer to a relation on equal, but on unequal terms, and it is in this relation that women are almost completely absorbed.

In recent years, women have placed themselves in direct opposition to men in aiming at equalization in all these respects, and occasionally they have succeeded, in such matters as personal position and economic independence, intellectual attainment and consciousness of self, in their freedom in society, and in their role in public life. A differentiation from men along party-lines, which emphasizes the solidarity of interests among women becomes noticeable as soon as their basic dissimilarity as over against men decreases with regard to their ways of life, their interest-orientation, and in terms of the law. These party-alignments [of women against men] are both cause and consequence of this development.

Very often it is in those comic figures of the emancipation, in those women whose ambition it is to be entirely masculine in their personality and their appearance, that we find the most passionate antagonism against men. This pattern is easily understood. The independence of women will develop to the same extent that their position, their value, and their qualities become equal to those of the men, to whom women had stood either in a relation of inferiority or, at any rate, of dissimilarity and, consequently, in a relation of dependence. It is apparent that this partial freedom makes those qualities more conspicuous and effective which women have in common with men, and which had to be suppressed previously in a relationship which confined the woman to a subordinate and complementary role. This is, then, an extraordinarily clear-cut case of group-formation on a higher level, which is based on the fact that members are brought together by a general concept. Previously, each of the members had been confined to a single group; now the new group emancipates them from this confining relationship.

This analysis is not altered by the fact that the movement for the emancipation of women goes in one direction with regard to working-class, and in an opposite direction with regard to middle-class women. The development of industry has given economic and social freedom to the proletarian woman—no matter how scanty her individual freedom may be. The girl works in a factory at an age at which she would still require the protected atmosphere of the parental home. The married woman works away from home, and this forces her to neglect her duties toward home, husband, and children. In this case, the woman is in fact released from this all-embracing tie which had been tantamount to her total subordination to the man, or to a complete separation of activities between them. This sociological fact is indeed undesirable and pernicious. But that does not change it, nor is it changed by the desire of the proletarian woman to have that "freedom" limited, and to have the possibility of again devoting herself to a greater extent to her family as a wife and mother. The same economic development has also affected women of the middle-class by separating from the home a great many domestic activities, both service and productive activities. Consequently, a very large number of women have been deprived of an adequate outlet for their energy, while they remain restricted in the main to the tasks of the home. These women long to have the freedom to engage in economic or other activities; in an emotional sense they feel just as removed from the special sphere of the home as the proletarian woman is externally. The difference in practical endeavor is a consequence of the difference between the social strata in which the separation from the home occurs. One class of women wants to return to the home, the other wants to escape it. These discrepancies are, nevertheless, compatible with interests which all women have in common: the rights of women with regard to marital laws, property laws, custody of children, etc., are of equal concern to both classes.

Moreover, the essential fact remains that the sociological isolation of the woman, the consequence of her absorption in the home, is being superseded in both classes by her separation from the home. This is the effect of modern industrialization. This separation may be too great or too little. But the independence which has been attained, or which is desired, accentuates the fact in either case that the modern woman is one who confronts the same practical situations and who has the same needs as other women. The general concept "woman" loses its purely abstract characteristics through the decline of the woman's complete preoccupation with the home. The general concept has become the guiding purpose of a cohesive group which is manifest in such details as charitable clubs organized exclusively by women and for women, leagues for the attainment of the rights of women, associations of women-students, women's congresses, and the organization of women for the realization of political and social goals.

The traditional identification of the concept "woman" with the special role of women in the home is extraordinarily close; it is much closer than the corresponding identification of the concepts "worker" or "trader" with their special roles. Hence today no one can predict either direction or limitation of the movement for the emancipation of women. However, this much can be said, that already many women as individuals are aware of their position at the "crossroads" of many groups. On one hand, they feel closely tied to the individuals and the activities which fill their personal life. But they are conscious, on the other hand, of their solidarity with all women.

In these cases [of labor, of employers, and of women] the more comprehensive, superordinated group is differentiated from, and supersedes, the more personal group-affiliations, which only contained certain potentialities for the formation of the superordinated group. But it may occur also that more coordinated groups are differentiated from one another. The guilds, for example, exercised complete supervision over the individual such that all of his activities would be regulated by the interests of the craft. If a boy had been accepted as an apprentice by a master, he became a member of the master's family. This meant that the individual's work in his trade became the center of his life in an unmistakable way. It included his political life and quite often his love life, too. Of the steps by which this amalgamation [between occupational activity and personal life] is dissolved, we need to deal only with the consequences of the division of labor.

OCCUPATIONAL ACTIVITY AND
THE DEVELOPMENT OF PERSONAL INTERESTS

ALL OTHER THINGS being equal, it can be said of everyone whose life is determined by a group of central, all-absorbing interests, that the influence of these interests on the person's life will diminish to the extent that they become less comprehensive. The occupation of an individual will appear to encompass the whole non-vocational world of ideas, even though it already involves many elements and a variety of ideas, because the consciousness of the individual is confined to that occupation. There need not exist any real relation between the particular occupation and the world outside. But an occupation which is not specialized necessarily requires a relatively rapid adjustment of ideas. This [intensified activity of the imagination] calls for a great deal of psychic energy[9] and the cultivation of other interests suffers accordingly. And as a consequence, these enfeebled interests are likely to become dependent—either by association or otherwise—upon the occupation which is of central concern to the individual.

This predominance of one interest at the expense of others may be compared to the emotional life of a man who is absorbed by a great passion. A man under its spell will establish some kind of association between his passion and even the most remote items which enter his awareness, though there is no substantive connection whatever between the two. And an equally absorbing, emotional identification will result in every occupation, which permits only a relatively small amount of mental energy to be invested in other aspects of life. This is one of the most important consequences of the division of labor. It is based upon the psychological fact, mentioned above, that within a given period of time—all other things being equal—the expenditure of mental energy increases with

9. To be sure, this is a symbolic expression that is indispensable in dealing with complicated psychological problems.

the frequency with which consciousness must shift from one idea or image to another. This shift of ideas is comparable in its consequences to the intensity of a passion. This is the reason—again all other things being equal—why an occupation which is not specialized rather than one which is, becomes the central concern in the life of a person and as such absorbs all his other interests. This is especially true of those historical periods in which the non-vocational life of the person lacked the colorful variety and changeable stimulations of modern times.[10]

It has to be added that one-sided occupations are usually of a rather mechanical nature. Therefore, they allow the individual to give more of his attention to non-vocational relations which have a value and an independence of their own.[11] This pursuit of separate but coordinate interests is furthered also by another consequence of the division of labor. This has to do with the formation of groups discussed above, i.e., groups which are based on an abstract concept and which are, thereby, separated from the particular group-affiliations of individuals. Associations between central and peripheral ideas and interests, although they resulted merely from psychological and historical causes, are usually considered essential and necessary. This view prevails until experience teaches us that there are persons who combine the same central ideas with different peripheral ones, or vice versa. If, then, the pursuit of an occupation had made all other interests in life dependent on it, it follows that this dependence had to decrease as the division of labor increased. For many similarities between the non-vocational interests of individuals were re-

---

10. Simmel refers throughout to all those interests and relations which lie outside an individual's principal occupation. I have translated this by the term "non-vocational," because the term "avocational" is too narrow in scope to render the author's meaning. Simmel does not refer to leisure-time activities, but to all activities outside the occupation. (R.B.)

11. This statement does not apply to those occupations which absorb all the strength and time of an individual and thereby lead to an atrophy of his entire mental energy.

vealed despite the differences between their occupations.

This pattern of development is exceedingly significant both for the inner make-up and the external conditions of people. A certain element in our personality is combined with a second, representing the specific elaboration of a characteristic which this second element shares with many other elements. At first, this combination takes hold of the second element in both its specific and its general character. But then a process of separation occurs, whereby the first element somehow combines with a third, which shares the general features of the second, though in an entirely different, specific elaboration. This process may have two wholly opposite consequences, depending upon how the general and the specific components of the second element blend with one another. If this blending is very intimate, the original combination of the elements will be completely destroyed.

This will often be the case, for example, where the moral life is tied to religion. For the individual his religion is as a rule the only religion; another religion is out of the question for him. He bases his moral convictions upon the special precepts of his religion. Subsequently, experience may convince him that the moral persuasion of other individuals is as genuine and as valuable as his own, but that it has been derived from completely different religious ideas. Only in rare cases is he likely to conclude, that morality is connected only with the religious mood in general, i.e., with what is common to all religions. He is more likely to draw a more far-reaching conclusion, namely that morality has nothing to do with religion at all. On this basis he will arrive at the view that morality is autonomous and he will not associate morality with the residual concept of the generally religious, which would be equally justified on logical grounds.

The case is different, if a man derives his satisfaction of having done his duty only from a kind of altruism which he continually associates with a painful suppression of his ego and with an ascetic self-torment. He sees that other people derive the same peace of mind and tranquillity of conscience from an altruism which is easily and freely exercised from a serene and unquestioning devotion to other. Yet, in this case he will not readily conclude that the inner peace and the feeling of being worthy, which he desires, have nothing to do with sacrifice for the other person. He is more likely to conclude only that altruism does not require sacrifices in an ascetic manner. He will feel that altruism may be practiced in a different way and still have the same success, if only its general characteristics are preserved.

The separation of vocational from all other interests in life, which was discussed previously in terms of the multi-plicity of occupations and its effects, constitutes a phenome-non half-way between the two examples given above; but in the main it will tend toward the first example. The very fact that a person has a vocation will always be linked to his life in its entirety. This formal or general characteristic will always be the center with reference to which many other aspects of his life are oriented. Still, this is a formal function of the vocation. As such it is compatible with the increasing separation of all vocational interests from one's personal life in the proper sense of that word.

The growing differentiation of occupations has taught the individual that all interests in life which lie outside a specific vocation, but which are similar in orientation, may be com-bined with different occupations. Consequently, such inter-ests must be independent from his specific occupation to a considerable degree. And the same independence of personal life from occupation results from the progressive differentia-tion of all non-vocational interests, which occurs in the course of cultural development. People in different occupa-tions may have the same non-vocational interests; and people who have different non-vocational interests may pursue the same occupation. This has the consequence of furthering the actual and the psychological separation of one from the other.

ASSOCIATION ON THE BASIS OF EXTERNAL
OR OF RATIONAL CRITERIA

WE HAVE OBSERVED the progress from a differentiation and combination [of individuals or ideas] according to external, schematic criteria to a differentiation and combination in terms of their real solidarity or affinity. This has an important analogy in the field of biological theory. Formerly, it was believed possible to solve the main problems of knowledge by combining large groups of living organisms according to the external symptoms of their kinship. However, a deeper and more accurate insight was gained by discovering morphological and physiological similarities in living organisms which were very different in appearance and which had been classified accordingly as different species. In this way the laws of organic life were arrived at. These laws were manifest at points far removed from one another on the scale of organic life. And the recognition of these laws brought about a unification of that which previously had been assigned, in terms of external criteria, to species of an entirely independent genesis. Here again a higher stage of development is indicated by the unification of what is homogeneous in terms of substantive criteria, and by its separation from heterogeneous associations.

For a group to be formed according to rational rather than mechanical and external criteria, it need not always gather its members from different structures. Hence, it need not always involve the creation of new groups. It may happen that exactly the same group is transformed from an external to a rational basis. In a group which is already in existence, a higher, more organic concept displaces the cruder and more accidental concept. And now the higher concept serves the basic function of holding the group together. This is approximately the pattern of development of the so-called iurati communiae in Rouen and other cities of northern France during the 12th century. These communiae were associations whose members were pledged to each other by oath. These associations were probably identical with the citizenry [Bürgerschaft] in all essentials, though not entirely and not on principle. For we learn from the constitutions of the *iurati communiae* that residents have committed a crime against the iurati and that some claim to belong to them under false pretenses. But further: the law stipulates that those who have lived in the city for a year and a day shall take an oath to the communiae. And those who wish to leave the latter must also leave the city. This community became in the end so powerful in every respect that it absorbed the entire citizenry, though not always quite voluntarily. Here we have, at first, a purely local, rather accidental symbiosis of townspeople. However, this symbiotic relationship is gradually permeated by an association which is deliberate, which is based upon a principle and directed by a purpose. Eventually, the entire complex constitutes a new and a higher type of group-formation, although neither its members nor the fact of their solidarity have been modified in any essential respect. A group which is organized rationally and on the basis of a central idea does not cut across the more primitive, or, if one will, the more natural group. In a way, it is rather a more sacred, a more spiritual form by means of which those who are unwitting members of a group [the town] find themselves together as if for the first time [in the iurati].

This formal development is repeated in the relation between colonies and their homeland, though this example is worlds removed from the one cited previously. European colonization, since Columbus and Vasco da Gama, suffered from the fact that territories were obligated to pay tribute, although they were remote from the homeland, and hardly derived any advantage from their affiliation with it. Meanwhile the homeland regarded the colonies merely as property. This form of association had no substantive justification and led to the secession of most of the colonies. The reason for secession was eliminated only when the idea of a Greater Britain arose, that the colony is but a province of the homeland with the same rights as any of the provinces geographically located inside the homeland. For, now the mode of association had changed from one in which the elements were welded together crudely and externally, to one in which they formed a bond of solidarity in a higher sense. Now the unity between homeland and colony was no longer rigid but elastic. The self-government of the colony was analogous to the relative independence of a limb on a body. Earlier examples showed a juxtaposition between group-formations based on schematic and on rational syntheses; this juxtaposition arose from new group-formations that cut across old affiliations. In this example [of homeland and colonies] the association based on a rational synthesis is not in juxtaposition to, but supersedes that based on a schematic synthesis.

EXTERNAL AND RATIONAL CRITERIA
OF GROUP-FORMATION ACCORDING TO
AN EVOLUTIONARY FRAME OF REFERENCE

THE SUCCESS of rational over superficial and schematic principles of group-formation accompanies the general progress of civilization. Yet this rational group-formation can be disrupted under certain circumstances, since it is not of an a priori character. The solidarity of the family may appear to be based on an external principle if it is compared to an association based on factual considerations. But the family will appear to be based on factual considerations in turn, if it is compared with groups based purely on numerical classifications, such as the companies of ten or a hundred in ancient Peru, in China, and in a large part of Europe in the early

Middle Ages. The social and political solidarity of the family and its collective liability for each of its members makes good sense; the rationality of this pattern becomes apparent, as the effects of heredity become known. But there is no national basis for always welding together in a group the same number of men treated as a unit—with regard to organization, compulsory military service, taxation, responsibility in case of a crime, etc. Nevertheless, where we are able to trace its development, such a group takes the place of the principle of kinship and represents a higher cultural level.

The justification for a group formed on the basis of numbers does not lie in the starting point, but in the goal, the *terminus ad quem*. As far as the starting point, the *terminus a quo*, is concerned, the family surpasses anything else as the basis for the differentiation and integration of groups. But groups formed on the basis of numbers are apparently better suited than the family for the achievement of a higher, national purpose, just because they are based on external characteristics, which can be more easily surveyed and organized. In ancient times the organization of armies was largely based on the clan or the family. In their Heroic Age the Greeks were fighting in phyle and phratry, the Germanic peoples in tribes and kinship-groups, and the ancient Scots in their clans, each of which could be identified by special insignia during the greater collective military expeditions. This organic structure was certainly useful in many respects: a great capacity of individual divisions to hold together, a stimulus to ambition, a certain relief of the supreme command from concern with the individual soldier and with the organization of each cadre. However, these advantages were obtained at a price. Frequent outbreaks of old prejudices and feuds between the clans would paralyze the unity of the whole movement. And among themselves the individual divisions were lacking in organic unity and cohesion to the same extent that each division possessed these qualities internally. Hence, the whole army was put together from its units in an inorganic manner, after all, despite the fact, or again just because of the fact that these units were organic in themselves.

The mechanical organization of later armies disregards the question of primary contacts among the members of a division. But from the point of view of the whole, this is a much more organic form of internal organization. The term "organic" is interpreted here as the uniform and purposive regulation of every smallest part by one single idea and the reciprocal determination between each element and every other. This more modern type of organization directly incorporates the individual. Its subdivisions and groupings ruthlessly cut across all other types of organization, and in so doing they destroy organic in favor of mechanic associations. However, this mechanical form of organization is incomparably more efficient than other forms in promoting the purpose which had also constituted the value of the more organic types of organization. The concept of *technology*, which is essential only in modern times, becomes relevant at this point. Modern techniques have succeeded in reaching more intellectual ends with more mechanical means, compared with the way of life of primitive periods which was less roundabout, more uniform and more instinctive.

This development is evident also in the principles of parliamentary election and in the way in which the organization of electoral districts cuts across already existing social groups. The representation of classes—as for instance the General States under Philipp the Fair which were the representatives of clergy, nobility, cities—appears at first to be natural and organic. This may be contrasted with the purely external organization of the electorate, such as the General States of the Netherlands under Philipp II of Spain, which were the local representatives of the individual provinces. The territorial division of the electorate involves the inclusion of so many different, sometimes irreconcilable interests, that it precludes a coherent expression of opinion through a single representative and his vote. The representation through interest-groups, which appears to be more rational than this mechanical and external method of representation, seems to succeed just in this point. But the case is actually the same as that of military organization. The individual groups, i.e., interest-groups with their representatives, are more organically constituted internally, but they stand side by side in a merely symbiotic relationship. Electoral procedures based on territorial units are more mechanical, to be sure, but the exclusively local election need not necessarily mean the representation of exclusively local interests. Indeed, this is precisely the technique for the organic integration of the whole. As a matter of principle the individual delegate represents the entire area. The ensuing separation into parties according to *political* tendencies implies then only differences of belief concerning the means by which the welfare of the nation is to be achieved. This is the only thing that matters, at least in the ideal case. The representation of estates or of interest-groups cuts across the merely external borderlines between areas by the force of its logic. But this partial rationality is deceptive; it obscures the fact that a mechanical subdivision on the basis of territorial units is in fact a technique which makes possible a much higher, organic synthesis of the whole.

CONCLUDING REMARKS

THIS IS THE PRINCIPAL PATTERN of the development of culture, which also comprises the sociological factors. Meaningful and profoundly significant institutions and behavior patterns are replaced by those which in themselves appear to be completely mechanical, external, and inanimate. But the latter have a higher purpose, which reaches beyond that of the earlier level of organization. And this higher purpose gives to the collective impact and to the consequences of institutions and behavior-patterns, an intellectual significance which is inevitably lacking in each single element. This is the characteristic of the modern soldier as over against the medieval knight, of factory work as over against handicraft work, of the modern levelling and uniformity of so many aspects of life, which were formerly left to the free and creative response of the individual.

On the one hand, organizations are too extensive and complex today to allow each of their members to express one idea completely, so to speak. Each of the members can have only mechanical significance without any meaning in themselves. Only as a member of the whole can he contribute his part toward the realization of an idea. On the other hand, the intellectual element in every activity is often differentiated so that the mechanical and the intellectual come to exist separately. For instance, the woman handling an embroidering machine engages in a much less imaginative activity than the woman embroidering by hand. The imaginative impulses of this activity have been transferred to the machine, they have become objectified. Thus, it is possible for social institutions, gradations, associations to become more mechanical and external, and yet, to serve cultural progress and the internal coherence of a whole group.

This is the case if a higher social purpose is at stake to which the individual must submit. This higher purpose will no longer permit them to retain the spirit and the rationale which under earlier social conditions gave to institutions and associations a terminus to their purposive activities. In this way we may explain the transition from the principle of kinship to the principle of social divisions by numbers, e.g., associations of ten, even though the latter principle involves an association of heterogeneous elements as opposed to the natural homogeneity of the family.

BOOKS PUBLISHED BY
The Free Press